THE PETERSEN HOUSE,

THE OLDROYD MUSEUM AND THE HOUSE WHERE LINCOLN DIED

The Petersen House,

The Oldroyd Museum and the House Where Lincoln Died

ALAN E. HUNTER

America Through Time®
ADDING COLOR TO AMERICAN HISTORY

America Through Time is an
imprint of Fonthill Media LLC
www.through-time.com
office@through-time.com

Published by Arcadia Publishing by arrangement with Fonthill Media LLC
For all general information, please contact Arcadia Publishing:
Telephone: 843-853-2070
Fax: 843-853-0044
E-mail: sales@arcadiapublishing.com
For customer service and orders:
Toll-Free 1-888-313-2665

www.arcadiapublishing.com

First published 2020

ISBN 978-1-63499-259-6

Typeset in 10pt on 13pt Sabon
Printed and bound in England

Acknowledgments

A volume such as this would not be possible without the many contributions of men, women, clubs, and organizations whose efforts laid the groundwork generations ago. Most notably among them is the National Park Service. Without their careful stewardship and meticulous documentation of the Petersen House and later, the house where Lincoln died, historians would be lost. In particular, I must thank Ka'mal McLarin, NPS Curator at the Frederick Douglass National Historic Site, Janet Folkerts, Museum Curator at the Vietnam War Memorial on the National Mall, and Laura Anderson, NPS Curator at the National Mall and Memorial Parks, for their careful assistance and patience during many hours spent pouring through the voluminous files at the house where Lincoln died and the NPS Museum Resource Center in Landover, Maryland. Bethanee Bemis of the Smithsonian Institution who takes the award for the coolest response to any research request ever when she said to "meet me at the Batmobile" when I visited the National Museum of American History. Most importantly, I must thank NPS Senior Ranger Roger Powell for sharing his vast knowledge and expertise from his many years spent at the house where Lincoln died—he is a true American treasure. His dedication to public service is unchallenged.

I am grateful for the Lincoln community of scholars and historians who are always willing to share their time and knowledge by continuing to assist researchers like me daily. Thanks to Laurie Verge, Curator of the Surratt House Museum and Colleen Puterbaugh, Research librarian at the James O. Hall Research Center in Clinton, Maryland, and to Dr. Diane Putney, whose knowledge of Ford's theatre is astonishing. And *bon voyage* to Jane E. Gastineau, recently retired Lincoln Librarian at the Lincoln Financial Foundation Collection in Allen County Public Library, Fort Wayne, Indiana, whose dedication and patience will be sorely missed.

Most of all, thanks to my wife, Rhonda, and children, Jasmine and Addison, for suffering through my obsession with Abraham Lincoln, the house where Lincoln died, and Osborn H. Oldroyd for the past decade. All of whom, by process of osmosis, have become quasi-experts in the field whether they wanted to or not. And thanks especially to those greater minds than mine for expanding my intellectual horizons by crystallizing their thoughts as if they were my own. On this subject, philosopher, essayist, lecturer, poet, and ardent Lincoln admirer and eulogist Ralph Waldo Emerson may have put it best when he said: "You become what you think about all day long." My friends, family and associates would recognize that in me.

COVER ILLUSTRATIONS

Front cover image: Pictured here for the first time ever, this vintage watercolor painting is titled *The Last Home of President Lincoln* and is signed by the artist T. Wakeman at bottom. The 7½-inch wide by 11-inch tall watercolor of the Petersen House dates from the period of 1866–1870. It was painted by Thomas Wakeman, a scene painter by profession. Not much is known about the artist, and Wakeman's story remains incomplete. Some biographies claim Wakeman, born in 1812, was an Englishman, while others describe him as a transplanted American living in Britain. Wakeman's British heritage (or residency) could explain the title's misnomer as Lincoln's home rather than the president's death site.

From the 1850s until his death in Rome in 1878, Wakeman visited the United States several times. He produced several hundred views of towns on the East Coast of America, including over forty noteworthy views from Boston south to Washington, D.C. His best known works include paintings of Robert E. Lee's Arlington House Mansion and High Street in Philadelphia. Most of his work in the U.K. was done in the Barking, Dagenham, East Ham area of suburban London. His trademark style is to stretch the vertical perspective making the buildings much taller than they really were. He was also known to fill his scenes with characters dressed in period clothing. In this view of the Petersen House, Wakeman has added a male figure standing on the platform above the curved brownstone steps as another man walks down the middle of the dirt street while reading a newspaper. Wakeman's view was most likely painted while seated in front of Ford's theatre, which was shuttered and used as U.S. War Department records storage at the time. It represents one of the earliest depictions of the house while the Petersen family was still residing there and before any of the familiar ornamentation was added to the exterior as identifiers. (*Author's collection*)

Back cover: One print of Lincoln's deathbed that illustrates the symbolic intent very explicitly is L. N. Rosenthal's lithograph *The Last Moments of Abraham Lincoln*. Here angels and George Washington look down on Lincoln from a bank of clouds hovering just above the bed. It is interesting that despite this print being the most blatantly symbolic of the Lincoln deathbed scenes, it is also one of the most accurate. The room is about the right size (even accounting for the bank of clouds), there are only twelve mourners—all of whom were likely there at Lincoln's death—the bed is accurate, and Herring's *Village Blacksmith* hangs upon the wall.

CONTENTS

INTRODUCTION

Although an oft-forgotten landmark in this city of landmarks, the house where Lincoln died in Washington, D.C., is as important as any historical waymark in the U.S. Not only is it noteworthy as the site where our first assassinated president, Abraham Lincoln, breathed his last, it is equally important as the site where the largest manhunt in our country's history began. For generations, it was the only shrine to the martyred president in our nation's capital city. Along the way, it would conjointly assume the mantel as a Civil Rights landmark. Contrary to its name, the house where Lincoln died is more than one dimensional.

Traveling through the streets of the national capital today, it is easy to experience the powerful geometry of the city's original plan. This glistening city of ideals is defined by its architecture—domes, obelisks, temples, cenotaphs, statuary, bridges, and radial avenues, all of which reinforce the importance of this seat of government's placement as the heights of the land. As novelist Charles Dickens observed in 1842, "It is sometimes called the City of Magnificent Distances, but it might with greater propriety be termed the City of Magnificent Intentions."[1]

The District can be a dizzying menagerie of addresses, titles, surnames, prefixes, suffixes, and directional abbreviations all designed to confuse the uninitiated. The capital's past is never far from its present. Perhaps no better illustration may be found than the unassuming looking three-and-a-half-story brownstone building on 10th Street directly across from the church-like theatre where America's greatest presidential tragedy took place.

Sometime around 10:30 p.m. on April 14, 1865, President Abraham Lincoln was shot in the head while watching a stage play at Ford's theatre. The hour is fitting from a biblical sense as it corresponds with the passage John 10:30, "I and the Father are one"—for at that moment, Lincoln began his secular transition from mortal to saint. Although the passage refers to Lazarus of Bethany, a.k.a. Saint Lazarus, it may easily be applied to Lincoln.

In the Gospel of John, the raising of Lazarus from the dead after four days is the climactic narrative of the seven signs, exemplifying once and for all the power of Jesus over the last and most irresistible enemy of humanity: death. For this reason, it is given a prominent place in the gospel. It could be said metaphorically that, like the "Righteous Lazarus," Lincoln would rise again in the curiously stacked little house on 10th Street.

As Lincoln's comatose body was carried from the theatre, fate intervened as it was carried up the curved Seneca sandstone steps and borne into a tiny bedroom at the back of an otherwise ordinary row house.[2] From that moment on, things were never the same on 10th Street. Within twenty-four hours of John Wilkes Booth's murderous act, Ford's Theatre was closed indefinitely and the Petersen family home was presaged by a sorrow that would never subside.

William Petersen, the homeowner who at first acquiesced to the use of his home as refuge for the dying president, was present at the beginning of the ordeal. He left the home and retreated to his nearby tailor shop at 480½ Pennsylvania Avenue to escape the pandemonium, only to return after the president's death and find his house overrun by souvenir hunters:[3]

> Thousands walked up and down 10th Street, moving as slowly as pallbearers as they eyeballed the theatre and the boarding house. Some were on a pilgrimage, others a treasure hunt. Souvenir hunters blotted blood from steps and chipped away at the brick buildings to retrieve slivers. Strangers tiptoed up to the Petersen's windows and peeked in. Artists drew the house from the street. Relic seekers knocked day and night.[4]

The assassination occurred on Good Friday, Lincoln died on Holy Saturday, and that Sunday became known colloquially as "Black Easter." Many Americans viewed the act as more than mere coincidence that assassination day was also crucifixion day. The meteoric posthumous growth of his reputation was influenced by the timing and circumstances of his death, which won for him a kind of saintly aura. Lincoln's shooting and death in the Petersen House were his first steps on the stairway to heaven. Just moments after he breathed his last breath in that house, Secretary of War Edwin Stanton kick-started the heavenward trip by stating, "Now he belongs to the angels."

Churches across the country were now faced with the difficult task of celebrating Easter and mourning the death of Lincoln at the same time. The resulting nationwide church services devoted to Lincoln on Easter Sunday began his posthumous religious transformation from man of the people to godlike status. Many Americans, north and south, came to believe that his death was the price this country paid for the bloodshed of the Civil War. In fact, it became the capstone for America's greatest internal sin: slavery.

The sermons preached on Easter Sunday 1865 painted a theologically enigmatic portrait of Abraham Lincoln. Barely twenty-four hours after his death, Lincoln's memory was already being defined as superhuman. Lincoln, as a symbolic figure, was revered not only by those who had supported him during his life, but now by all Americans, and soon by the whole world.

Within forty-eight hours of his passing, the association of Lincoln's character with American tradition began. The clergy, alongside their biblical images of Moses and martyrdom, now invoked the images of Lincoln and the founding fathers. In addition to grouping the Emancipation Proclamation and the Declaration of Independence as sacred texts, these sermons also established a link between Lincoln and the nation's first President George Washington.

The timing and tragic nature of Lincoln's death underscored the accomplishments of his life. Lincoln quickly became a central figure—perhaps the central figure—in the unfolding epic of America as a nation post-1865. Who else but Lincoln, the rough-hewn man forged on the prairies of Indiana, Kentucky, and Illinois, could have seen us through the sectional conflict pitting brother against brother? The plain speaker—unpolished, unschooled, and untutored—somehow managed to master a situation that was in his own words "piled high with difficulty." He did so with a rhetorical mastery that no other American political figure has come close to matching since.

Generations of schoolchildren were taught to memorize two things: the Pledge of Allegiance and the Gettysburg Address. Lincoln's image graces both our paper money and our coinage. Lincoln is referred to as Father Abraham, Honest Abe, and the Great Emancipator. Therefore, it should come as no surprise to even the most casual observer that a visit to the Petersen House—the house where Lincoln died—became an *ersatz* religious experience.

The events of that tragic night are well known. This volume can promise to add little to that narrative. The focus of this book will be to delineate the history of the property, house, and museum through the use of photographs and images beginning with the earliest days of the district's timeline. Once it was determined that the house was no longer a home, a movement commenced to convert it into a shrine—a national shrine not only honoring Abraham Lincoln but also to honor civil rights and racial equality.

As the reader flips through the pages of this volume, it becomes evident that most views are of the east front, street elevation as seen from the Ford's Theatre doorway where Abraham Lincoln was removed. So, although many of these photos appear similar in composition, they are all valuable tools designed to tell the story of Lincoln's final earthly journey as viewed from threshold to conclusion.

Henrik Ibsen, the Norwegian playwright considered to be "the father of realism" and one of the founders of modernism in theatre, once said "A thousand words leave not the same deep impression as does a single deed." Napoleon Bonaparte stated: "A good sketch is better than a long speech." Leonardo da Vinci wrote that a poet would be "overcome by sleep and hunger before [being able to] describe with words what a painter is able to in an instant." So, if it is true that a picture is worth a thousand words, the images on the following pages will convey each meaning or essence more effectively than a mere verbal description.

THE HOUSE WHERE LINCOLN DIED

The death of Abraham Lincoln in the William Petersen House on April 15, 1865 might be considered our country's first national calamity. Until that time, George Washington was revered as the American ideal. In this CdV (*carte de visite*) photograph from 1865, Washington's godlike status is illustrated by his welcoming Lincoln into the kingdom of heaven. While Washington was the founding father of the United States, Lincoln saved the nation from division and collapse, linking the two inextricably together forever. (*Author's collection*)

Above: The decision to locate the Federal Capital in its present location is generally credited to two men: George Washington and Thomas Jefferson. Washington, who had spent most of his life surveying nearly all of known America, believed that the nation would inevitably expand westward and that the Potomac could be linked to the interior by canals and great waterways like the Ohio. Pierre Charles L'Enfant, a French-American military engineer, was appointed by President Washington in 1791 to plan the new "Federal City" under the supervision of three commissioners. L'Enfant's grid plan specified locations for two buildings, the "Congress House" (the United States Capitol) and the "President's House" (the "White House" or "Executive Mansion"). (*Photo courtesy the Library of Congress*)

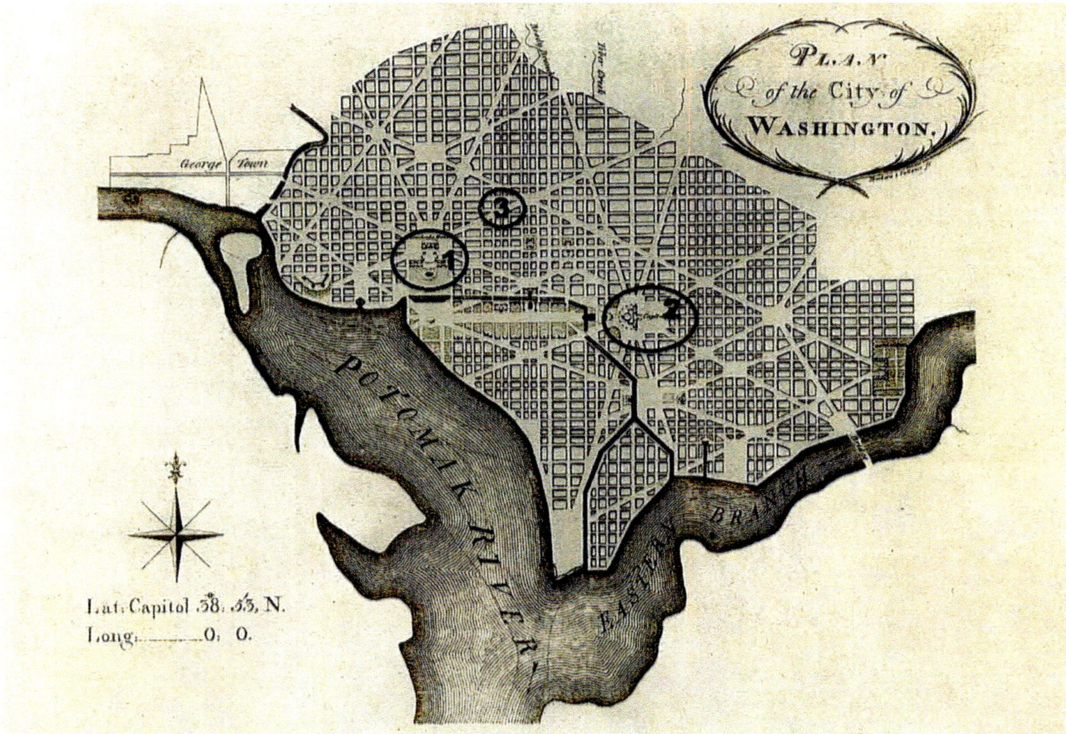

Previous page, below: L'Enfant's map from March 1792 was titled "Plan of the City of Washington." Following the streets and squares within Major Pierre Charles L'Enfant's plan for the capital city in 1791, former farms and tracts of land were divided up for sale to encourage development. The city's earliest streets cut through thick woods, the only deforested areas being those surrounding public buildings. No. 1 represents the White House and No. 2 the Capitol Hill. No. 3 on this map represents the undeveloped future site of the Petersen House and Ford's Theatre. (*Photo courtesy the Library of Congress*)

Above left: In 1703, a land patent was granted to Ninean Beall of Upper Marlboro, Maryland, for a tract of land that included the future Petersen House property. Col. Ninian Beall (1625–1716) is remembered for his long red hair and towering height of 6 feet 7 inches (remarkable for his time). Beall is considered a founding father of the Georgetown area. (*Photo courtesy the Library of Congress*)

Above right: The southern half of Lot 14 in Square 347, the future site of the Petersen House, was owned from 1793 to 1797 by James Greenleaf, a real estate investor from Massachusetts. The building lot (current lot 823) is 25 feet wide by 100 feet deep and the Petersen House, at approximately 25 feet wide and 80 feet deep, occupies most of it. Greenleaf also owned several neighboring lots. After forming a partnership with two land speculators (Robert Morris and John "James" Nicholson), Greenleaf gained control of 6,000 lots. Ultimately, the syndicate reneged on payments for the lots and went bankrupt in 1797 and the lots reverted to the Federal government. (*James Greenleaf painting by Gilbert Stuart, oil on canvas—Portland Art Museum, Portland, Oregon*)

Above: A deed, found in the archives of the National Park Service at Ford's Theatre, issued to William A. Petersen, states that the property was purchased from Abner and Mary Ann Young for $850 on February 5, 1849. The Petersen House, familiarly known as "The House Where Lincoln Died," is a 38-foot-tall "three-story-plus-basement" Greek Revival row house built that same year. "The Petersen House is a sturdy three-story red-brick, constructed to conform with the small lot on which it is situated and similar in design to houses built by moderate-income families during the mid-19th Century."[1] This newspaper woodcut view of the house dates from April of 1865 and depicts the building draped in mourning by a design that would henceforth be known as the "Lincoln drape." From 1844 to 1853, the Petersen House address was listed as "10th West between E and F North." From 1855 to 1858, the house was given the address of 455 10th Street, from 1858 to 1869 the building's address was 453 10th Street. Finally, the Petersen boarding house was numbered "516 10th N.W." in 1869, and remains so today. (*Author's collection*)

Previous page, below: Ford's Theatre as it would have looked in 1865. Note the ghostly image of an unknown man in a top hat posed on the plank sidewalk behind the wooden carriage step that guests, including Abraham Lincoln, would have used to descend from their carriages. The site, originally constructed as the First Baptist Church of Washington in 1833, was purchased by John T. Ford in 1861 after the congregation moved to a new building. Ford renovated the structure into a theater that he first called "Ford's Athenaeum." Located directly across the street from the Petersen House, the theatre was destroyed by fire in 1862, rebuilt, and became forever known as "Ford's Theatre" after the assassination of Abraham Lincoln there on April 14, 1865. (*Author's collection*)

Above: Currier & Ives lithograph titled *The Assassination of President Lincoln at Ford's Theatre, Washington, D.C. April 14th, 1865.* This graphic image identifies John Wilkes Booth as the "Assassin," Lincoln as "The President," with "Maj. Rathbone" lunging at the murderer as "Miss Harris" and "Mrs. Lincoln" watch in horror. These prints were first sketched by an artist on paper, then etched on lithographic limestone or a metal plate. Once printed, each lithograph was hand colored, a separate artist employed to apply each tint, and finally clipped to a clothesline to dry. Photography was in its infancy at the time of the Lincoln tragedy, and during the first generation after the crime, lithography, with its ability to add color to an otherwise colorless template, was considered to be the gold standard of imaging. (*Photo courtesy the Library of Congress*)

Right: CdV photograph of John Wilkes Booth as he appeared at the time of the assassination. This photo features a partial signature affixed by the actor at the top. The signature is mis-cut as it was signed in the photographer's studio while a part of a larger uncut sheet of multiple photos before being cut and glued to the cardboard mat. Booth was considered the most handsome actor of his day and reportedly the second-most photographed man in the country, behind only Abraham Lincoln. Photos like these were collected and traded like baseball cards a century later. (*Author's collection*)

Above: An 1865 painting titled *Lincoln Borne By Loving Hands*, created by German-born artist Carl Bersch. On the night of the assassination, Bersch was seated on his 10th Street balcony sketching a torchlight parade celebrating Robert E. Lee's surrender five days earlier. The artist witnessed the scene depicting the mortally wounded president being carried by soldiers from the theatre and into the Petersen House. "My balcony being twelve or fourteen feet above the sidewalk and street, I had a clear view of the scene, above the heads of the crowd. I recognized the lengthy form of the President by the flickering light of the torches, and one large gas lamp-post on the sidewalk. The tarrying at the curb and the slow, careful manner in which he was carried across the street, gave me ample time to make an accurate sketch of that particular scene."[2] Bersch quickly sketched the tragedy as it unfolded and later turned it into this painting, now on display at Ford's Theatre National Historic Site. (*Author's collection*)

Below: Moody, Tearful Night bronze by sculptor Richard Masloski. The title of the work is taken from the Walt Whitman poem about Lincoln's death, "When Lilacs Last in the Dooryard Bloom'd." It depicts Surgeon General Joseph K. Barnes cradling the head and shoulders of Lincoln as soldiers from Thompson's Battery C, Independent Pennsylvania Artillery (Jacob J. Soles, William Sample, Jabes Griffiths, and John Carey) carry the dying President into the Petersen House. This sculpture, one of only seven made, is on display at the entrance to the genealogy room of the Allen County Library in Fort Wayne, Indiana. It was a gift to the library, home of the Lincoln Financial Collection, from Ian and Mimi Rolland. (*Photo by author*)

Right: Newspaper woodcut from April 15, 1865 entitled "Conveying the President from the Theatre to the House of Mr. Petersen." The image, signed by the artist "Risdon," depicts the gravely wounded Lincoln being carried to the bed in Private William Clark's room in the rear of the Petersen House. As he watched the bearers wind their way through the crowd toward his home, William Petersen, standing on the curved stairway, shouted, "The President is coming," before rushing into his house and disappearing during the chaos. He was not seen again until morning.[3] A distraught Mary Lincoln, hands covering her face, is escorted by Clara Harris to the right of the bed as the unconscious president is lifted on to the bed. The bed was too short for the 6-foot 4-inch Lincoln and he was placed upon it diagonally, his head positioned towards the door. (*Author's collection*)

Below: Newspaper woodcut from April 15, 1865 entitled "House of Mr. Petersen, opposite Ford's Theatre, Washington, D.C., Where the President Died. From a sketch by A. Berghaus."[4] The image depicts the Petersen House as the president lay dying inside. The stairway to the door is guarded by armed Federal soldiers with rifles crossed, buttressed by soldiers on horseback, while still more soldiers keep curious onlookers away at the point of their bayonets. This view is unique because, like the Ford's Theatre image previously revealed, it pictures the wooden carriage step used by the residents of 10th Street. Aside from the curved sandstone steps leading to the door of the Petersen House, this contemporary view also captures the distinctive spider-web window on the door immediately to the right (north) of the stairway. The door leads to a space, formerly an alley, that was converted into an enclosed passageway when a three-story row house to the north of the Petersen House was built sometime prior to 1865. This paneled door and its Chinoiserie-inspired opening in the top third remains unchanged and largely unnoticed to this day. (*Photo courtesy National Park Service Ford's Theatre Historic Site archives*)

Above: This sketch, titled *Deathbed of President Lincoln*, was made on scene April 15, 1865 by artist Herman Faber.[5] One of two sketches by Faber made just after the president's body was removed, this view is unusual because it shows the physicians actively working on the president. Used bandages, mustard plasters, and a used wash basin full of murky water rests on the floor and the image of a woman carrying in a fresh basin full of water can be seen in the doorway. Secretary of the Navy Gideon Welles is seated by the bed, Secretary of War Edwin Stanton stands behind him, and Robert Todd Lincoln, dressed in his military uniform, sits in a chair crying profusely at his dying father's feet. This is the only deathbed image depicting Mr. Lincoln with a bandaged head. (*Photo courtesy Meserve-Kunhardt Collection*)

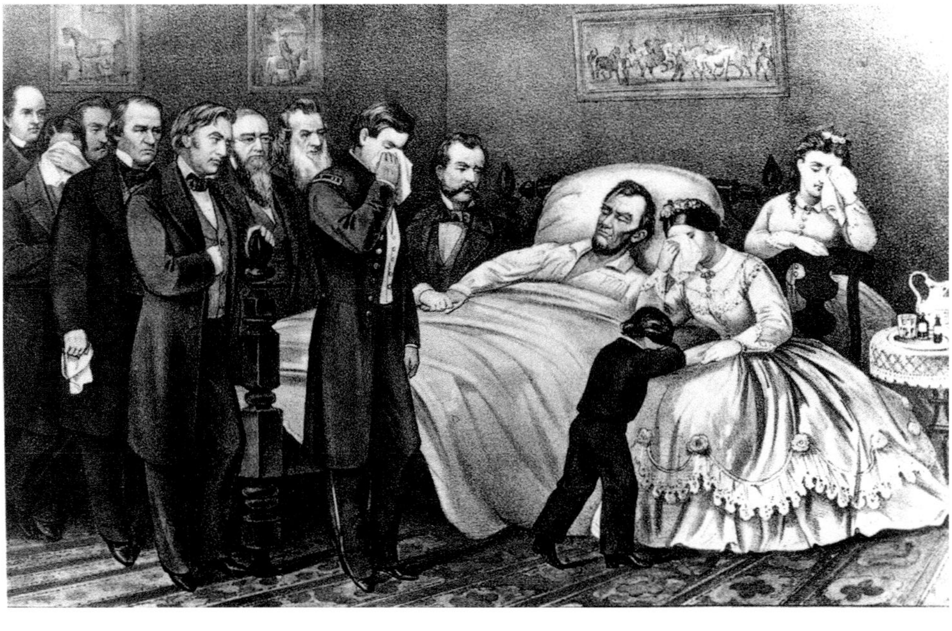

Previous page, below: This Currier & Ives print, titled *Death of President Lincoln at Washington, D.C. April 15th, 1865* features a copyright date of April 26, 1865. This print depicts a grief stricken Mary Lincoln seated at her husband's bedside which, although she was ultimately banished from the room by Secretary Stanton, is accurate. The inaccuracy arises with the inclusion of Tad Lincoln in the print. Tad, posed sobbing into his mother's lap, was never called to his father's deathbed despite Mary's pleadings that the boy be fetched from the White House. Mary believed that her dying husband would awake if he could simply hear Tad's voice. (*Photo courtesy Lincoln Financial Collection Indiana State Museum Indianapolis*)

Over a dozen different images of Abraham Lincoln's death at the Petersen House were produced in the years following the tragedy. As Lincoln's legend grew, so did the room in which he died and the number of witnesses present there. This 1868 print, by artist Alonzo Chappel features an astounding forty-seven witnesses crammed into the tiny room (18 feet 2 inches by 9 feet 11 inches).[6] In succeeding years, historians consider Chappel's work to be an aggregated depiction of the seven-hour vigil rather than a representation of the moment of the president's death. Although all of the people depicted in Chappel's work were present at one time or another during the night, it is doubtful that the group in its entirety could be comfortably fitted into the entire ground floor of the house where Lincoln died, let alone the death room. (*Photo courtesy Chicago Historical Society*)

Alonzo Chappel was meticulous in his documentation for his mammoth painting he titled *The Last Hours of Lincoln*. The artist went so far as to have several of his subjects pose for photographs at Mathew Brady's studio for accuracy, some in the exact poses later depicted in his painting. *Left to right*: Robert Todd Lincoln, Andrew Johnson, Secretary of the Treasury Hugh McCullough, Edwin Stanton, and Gideon Welles. Can you find these men in Chappel's painting? (*Photo courtesy Chicago Historical Society*)

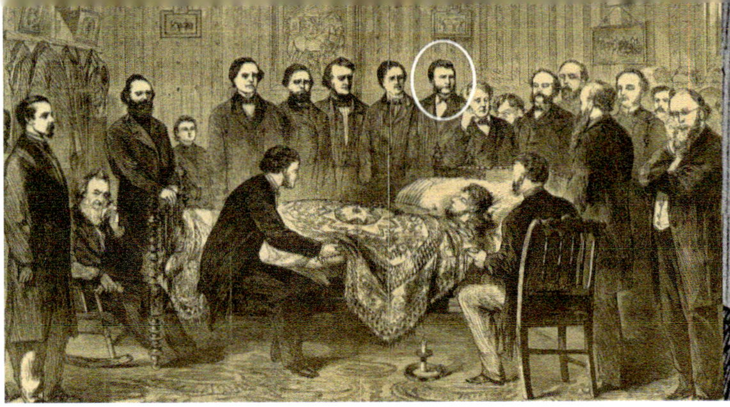 

Above: This drawing by Albert Berghaus appeared in the April 29 issue of *Frank Leslie's Illustrated*. The artist enlisted some of Petersen's boarders to identify the individuals present during Lincoln's final moments and to help determine their placement in the room. His sketch erroneously included homeowner William Petersen who was not present at the time but nonetheless included as recognition for his help in recreating the scene. The cutaway image (at right) survives as the only known identifiable portrait of William Petersen. Along with Petersen, the drawing also pictures Petersen House boarders Thomas Proctor, Henry Safford, and brothers Henry and Julius Ulke, who were also not present in the room at the time of Lincoln's death. (*Photo courtesy National Park Service Ford's Theatre Historic Site archives*)

Below: After Lincoln's body was removed and the visitors departed, Petersen House boarder Julius Ulke set up his camera and photographed the bedroom. This graphic image shows a woven coverlet strewn across the bed and a pillow soaked with Lincoln's blood. Ironically, assassin John Wilkes Booth had rested in this same bed a month previous while visiting his friend and fellow actor Charles Warwick, who was renting the room at the time. Ulke, who had furnished hot water to the doctors throughout the night, and his brother, Henry, operated a portrait studio at 1111 Pennsylvania Avenue, N.W., around the corner from their boarding house. The brothers were accomplished entomologists, maintaining one of the largest collections of beetles in existence. Historians note that the Ulkes' room in the Petersen House was likely unfit for the president due to the many beetle specimens and scientific instruments held there. The Ulkes' beetle collection was in the house on the night that Lincoln died and was later donated to the Carnegie Museum. (*Photo courtesy Meserve-Kunhardt Foundation*)

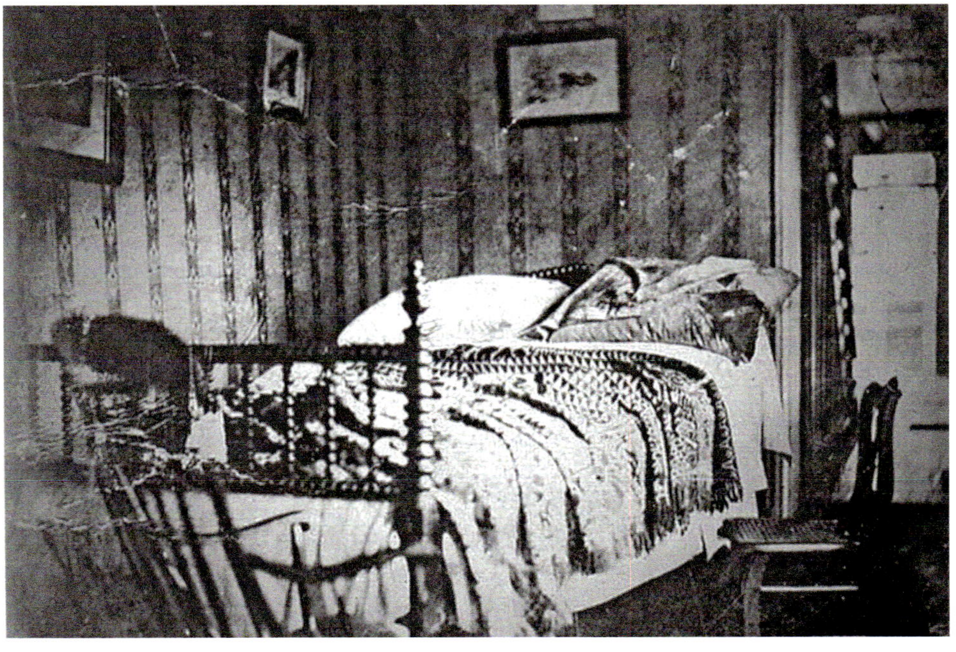

Three newspaper woodcut images of the Petersen House as it appeared in the 1880s. The post assassination years were not happy ones for the Petersen family. With the close of the Civil War, William Petersen's lucrative uniform business skidded to a halt. Ford's theatre closed, never to reopen, so no longer could the family rent rooms to transient actors and soldiers. By 1867, William had closed his Pennsylvania Avenue tailor shop and moved his business into the English basement below his 10th Street home. Soon, Petersen began to imbibe in a legal over-the-counter tonic known as "laudanum," a tincture of opium and alcohol, that could be deadly if improperly used. On June 18, 1871, William Petersen died from an overdose of laudanum while seated on a bench in front of the iconic red castle of the Smithsonian Institution. While some newspapers labeled it a suicide, the family insisted that it was an accidental overdose. His wife, Anna, died exactly four months later. Within a month of Anna's death, her furniture and personal possessions were sold at auction to settle their estate. These lots included the Lincoln deathbed frame and mattresses for $80. (*Author's collection*)

Louis Frederick Schade (1829–1903), a German-American newspaper publisher, purchased the Petersen House in February of 1879 for $4,500. According to the deed, the purchase was actually between the Petersen heirs and Schade's wife, Anna. The deed offers a detailed description of the property: "Known and distinguished as the South half of lot numbered fourteen in square numbered three hundred and forty seven fronting twenty-five feet on 10th Street and running back the same width to an alley." Although not listed as the property owner, Louis Schade did act as his own notary public on the document. The Schades used the upper floors of the home as living quarters and the "English" basement for Louis' pro-immigration newspaper, *The Washington Sentinel*, which had previously been located at 935 E. NW Street less than a block away from the HWLD. (*Library of Congress*)

Above: A 3¼-inch by 4-inch (known as American size) photographic image of the Louis Schade home on a "magic lantern" glass slide designed to be projected by a light source against a blank wall. It consists of two sheets of glass, one of which features the image and the other which acts as a cover to protect it from dust and scratches, both bound all around by a black paper tape. The slide is identified on one side as "T.H. McAllister, Manufacturing Optician. 49 Nassau Street, New York" and marked "Private collection of George S. Paine" with a handwritten description of the HWLD on the other. The view pictures the establishment known as "Mrs. Whiting's Millinery" next door at 518 North 10th St. The slide appears in the February 1887 issue of T. H. McAllister's "Catalogue and price list of stereopticons, dissolving view apparatus, magic lanterns, and artistically-colored photographic views on glass." (*Author's collection*)

Previous page, below: In this *c.* 1888 image, the upper floor windows of the Schade residence stand wide open, curtains flapping in the breeze, as the English basement office of Schade's newspaper are closed to business. The *Sentinel* was published every Saturday at 5 cents per week. Schade mostly used his paper as an outlet for his own political views in support of more lenient immigration policies. Schade, a former assistant librarian at the Smithsonian Institution and Census Bureau official, had been very active in Democratic politics and, ironically, the presidential campaign of Stephen A. Douglas against Abraham Lincoln. After the 1860 election was over, Schade took up the practice of law and became famous for defending Confederate Army Major Henry Wirz, commandant of notorious Andersonville prison in Georgia, in a war crimes trial in 1865. (*Author's collection*)

Above left: This postcard provides a view of the Petersen House from around 1889 during the time when Louis Schade was publishing his newspaper in its lowest level. The publisher placed a large shield-shaped sign to the right of the home's main entrance, above the spider-web door of the covered alleyway, with the *Washington Sentinel* name emblazoned upon it. To avoid confusion, Schade also painted the *Washington Sentinel* name on the sash header above the window of the basement office. A testament to the intrusiveness of visits by well-meaning, yet inconvenient, Lincoln pilgrims may also be deduced by the fact that every window shutter is closed up tight to prying eyes. (*Author's collection*)

Above right: This image, from around 1890, pictures a pair of young boys (likely Schade's sons, Hermann and Frederick) standing in front of the family home. According to an August 17, 1879 *New York Herald* account, the first permanent public marker placed on the exterior of the Petersen House was a marble tablet created by Washington, D.C., artist Charles Rousseau in August of 1879. The tablet was inscribed, "Abraham Lincoln died in this house twenty-two minutes past 7 a.m., April 15, 1865." While no evidence survives to explain why (or how) the tablet was placed there, it may be assumed that Rousseau was commissioned by Schade to create and place it there to alleviate the near constant inquiries from bothersome door-knocking tourists. The February 24, 1883 edition of the *Washington Sunday Star* reported that Schade's wife, Anna, "found their lives continually interrupted as tourists knocked at their door, displaying all sorts of bad manners and acting as if they were inspecting a public museum." (*Author's collection*)

Above left: This image, from the late 1880s, is important because it offers a view of the business next door to the HWLD at 518 10th St. NW. The "ghost sign" remains visible, reading "Mrs. Whiting's Millinery Steam Dyeing and Scouring" above the people posed standing on the balcony featuring a distinctive wrought-iron railing. A new business, "Dundore's Employment Bureau," has moved in and the windows are covered with job notices and a large poster for a baseball game at Athletic Park, home of the American Association Washington Nationals. The ballpark was located several blocks away at S Street NW (south); 9th Street NW (east); T Street NW (north); and 10th Street NW (west). By 1889, the ballpark was demolished and the block cut into lots for new residences and education-related buildings. The poster was displayed because the ballpark, no doubt, was a major employment source for temporary workers during the summertime. This building is important in the HWLD saga simply because of the transient nature of the businesses located there that literally fueled the fear of fire destroying the HWLD and the collection housed within for the next 100 years. (*Library of Congress*)

Above right: This postcard provides another view of the Petersen House during the time when Louis Schade was publishing his newspaper in its lowest level. The view is noteworthy for a couple of reasons. Louis Schade can be seen in the lower window at left dressed in his apron and shirtsleeves working, most likely setting typeface, for his newspaper. Also, a portrait of the sixteenth president has been placed above Rousseau's marble tablet and another larger sign at street level reading: "In this building Abraham Lincoln Died on the morning of April 15, 1865." The view dates from around 1890 (shortly before the Schade family sold the house) and features an early image of the Logan Cafe to the right of the Petersen House. The Logan Cafe, located next door at 518 North 10th St., first opened in 1887 and was formerly known as the Forsythe Cafe. (*Author's collection*)

Above left: By 1893, when this amateur cabinet photo was taken, the Schade family had become so frustrated with visitors scolding them for allowing their children to play in the death room that they moved away. The December 17, 1887 edition of the *Star* reported that "Mr. Schade and his family have to suffer considerable annoyance by reason of occupying a house with such historic associations.... 'We always show those who apply politely the room where the President died. Sometimes the visitors offer money but we do not allow even our servant to accept it.' Mr. Schade some time ago received an offer for the house, but refused it because he understood the intention was to make a showplace of it." That year, Schade was persuaded to lease it to the Memorial Association of the District of Columbia. Three years later, he sold it to the Association for $30,000 ($850,000 in 2020 dollars). In this image, the *Sentinel* sign above the window remains, but the shield-shaped banner near the door has been removed and the lettering on Rousseau's marble tablet has become faded from the sun. Next door, "Mrs. Whiting's Millinery" is still in operation and has added an awning above the door touting "Bleaching-Millinery" services. (*Author's collection*)

Above right: The Memorial Association of the District of Columbia was formed on March 18, 1892 to properly mark (and preserve) locations of historical importance in the capital city in preparation of the approaching national centennial celebration of 1900. The D.C. Memorial Association formed committees to pick sites they believed would be of particular interest to the returning Civil War veterans. The association believed that the city had changed so drastically since the old soldiers had been encamped there that they decided these sites should be given numbered markers for identification. The result of the association's toil was a handsome booklet published in 1893 titled *Historic Washington*. At over sixty pages long, the booklet sold for a dime and contained brief sketches of historic buildings on the Memorial Association's watch list, including the district's oldest school house, Octagon House, Van Ness House, Kalorama, Beale House, Union Hotel, Tudor Place, Washington Monument, and Arlington House among others. It should be noted that while the "The House Where Lincoln Died" was the cover subject, it was not mentioned on any of the pages inside. (*Library of Congress*)

Above: The first major step in the association's legitimacy came when they leased the Petersen House at 516 10th Street NW for use as their office and headquarters. The association experienced a shock to their system when, at 9:30 a.m. on Friday June 9, 1893, three floors inside Ford's theatre collapsed. The building, located just yards away from the Petersen House, was in use by the Office of Records and Pensions run by the War Department. This photo pictures Ford's Theatre around the time of the disaster. (*Library of Congress*)

Previous page, below: This photo shows the interior of Ford's Theatre after the collapse that killed twenty-two employees instantly and injured 105 more (three more would eventually die of their injuries). Most were crushed by desks and filing cabinets that fell into the void on top of them. The theatre would stand in place, shuttered and untouched, used only for government storage, for the next thirty-one years until 1924 when it would be revisited as a place to memorialize President Lincoln. (*Photo from author and former Ford's theatre ticket taker John E. Buckingham Sr.'s 1894 book "Reminiscences and Souvenirs of The Assassination of Abraham Lincoln," author's collection*)

Above left: The Memorial Association's intention was to turn the Petersen House into a shrine to Lincoln. In 1893, there were only a couple statues dedicated to Abraham Lincoln available for veterans to visit in the capital city. The association forged an alliance with Civil War Veteran Osborn H. Oldroyd, the great Lincoln collector whose collection was previously on display in the Lincoln Homestead in Springfield, Illinois. Oldroyd had recently been removed from the Illinois shrine by a change in the Governor's office. He was persuaded to move his collection into the house where Lincoln died. This image represents the earliest days of Oldroyd's tenancy and shows the American flag displayed from the center top floor window, which would become an ever-present fixture of Oldroyd's museum for the next three decades (note the employee standing on the balcony of the second floor millinery next door). (*Author's collection*)

Above right: A *c.* 1893 postcard image of the house where Lincoln died after the Schade family had vacated the property and leased it to the Memorial Association of the District of Columbia. The shadow of Schade's shield-shaped newspaper sign can be seen next to the entry door and the sign above the window has now been painted over. As yet, there is no sign on the railing denoting the museum's placement inside the building, the flag is retracted and the upper floor windows are shuttered. The flagpole was unattached at the time of this photo, but would soon become a permanent fixture on the face of the landmark. (*Author's collection*)

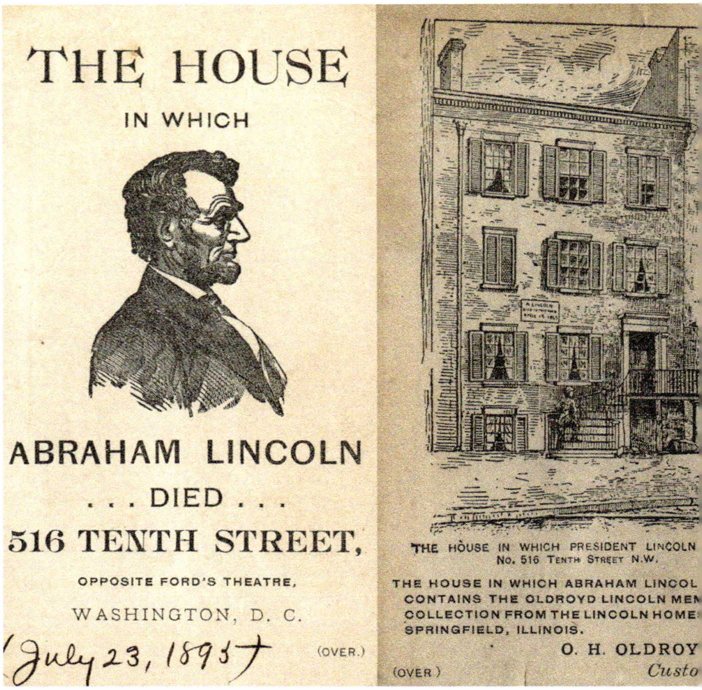

Above left: This cabinet photo dates from around 1894 and pictures Lincoln Museum curator Osborn Oldroyd posed leaning against the railing of the house where Lincoln died. During the earliest years of Oldroyd's occupancy, the doorway was draped with four large American flags draped as bunting in the fashion of an awning above the door and cascading down on each side of the entryway. A small metal sign was attached to the center panel of the door reading: "Visitors Received. 9 to 12 a.m.—1 to 4 p.m. Daily. Admission 25 ¢." For a time, the metal railing remained unadorned. The curator's wife, Lida Oldroyd, can be seen looking north out of the uppermost floor of the building, which served as the living quarters of the family. She is likely gazing out towards the family's church, the First Congregational Church, located one-and-one-half blocks due north of the museum at 10th and G Street NW. (*Meserve-Kunhardt Collection*)

Above right: Here is an early handout advertising the Oldroyd Museum in the house where Lincoln died. On October 17, 1893, the new "Lincoln Memorial Collection" was opened to the public. A veritable who's who of Washington high society flocked to 10th Street for the dedication of the new museum in the former Petersen House. According to the October 14, 1893 editions of both the *Evening Star* and *Washington Post*, the Oldroyd memorial collection consisted of over 2,500 items, including over 1,000 biographies along with countless photographs, busts, badges, furniture, medals, and even a rail reputedly split by Lincoln himself. This particular pamphlet, pictured here front and back, is dated July 23, 1895. (*Author's collection*)

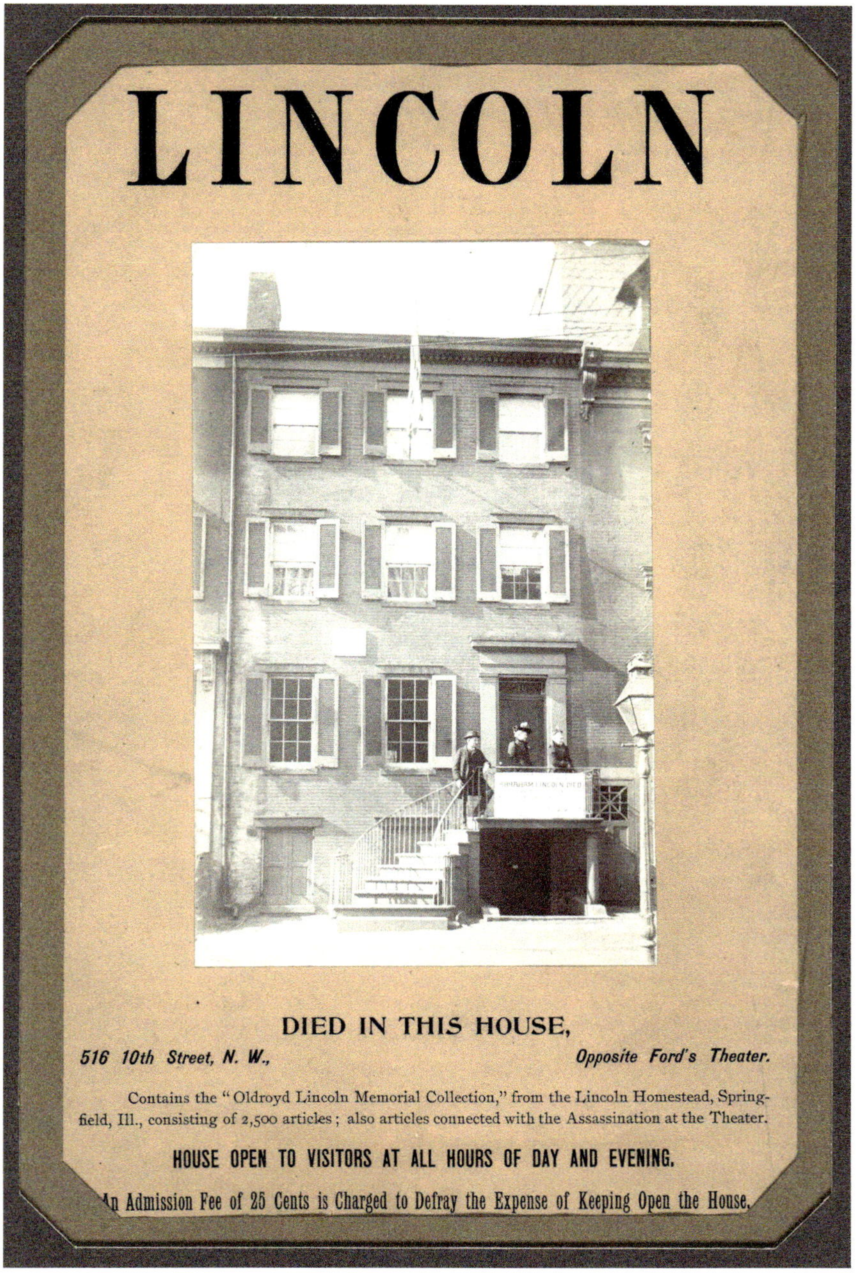

A *c.* 1896 photo poster for the Oldroyd Collection displayed inside the house where Lincoln died. The Oldroyd family (*left to right*: Osborn, his daughter, Daisy, and wife, Lida) posed behind the newly installed sign advertising the collection. These signs would remain, in various textual forms, attached to the railing first by Oldroyd, then by the U.S. Government, for the next 125 years. This image also offers an excellent view of the HWLD with all of the window shutters thrown open and held in place by "Rat Tail Shutter Dog" style iron stays attached to the building. These cast-iron stays were augmented by "Bullet Catches" attached to the building in each shutter corner designed to further anchor each shutter tightly to the building. (*Library of Congress*)

Above: A *c.* 1898 large sized (13¾-inch wide by 10¾-inch tall) cabinet photo picturing a group of doctors and clerks from the U.S. Surgeon General's office on the steps in front of a sign reading: "This House in Which Abraham Lincoln, Died, Contains 2500 Relics Relating to the Martyred President, Most of Them from his homestead at Springfield Illinois. Open Daily Except Sunday 9 to 12 m. 1 to 4 p.m. Tuesday and Friday 8 to 10 p.m. Admission 25 ¢." There is a separate metal sign on the door reading: "Visitors Received. 9 to 12 a.m. to 4 p.m. Admission 25 ¢." The men are identified on back (in no particular order) as Dr. Homer E. Nowlin (1869–1910), Dr. Frances E. Park (1876–1899), Albert G. Yount (1843–1924), R. M. Patrick, Jonathan H. Thomas, William H. Collings (1849–1924), Thomas Harris Jones (1861–1908), Cassius M. Puntenney (1858–1915), Arthur Schatz (died 1928), David K. Sargent, C. H. Bliss, and Philip H. Cass (1869–1912). All three of the men posed on the left side of the photo are proudly displaying G.A.R. badges on the lapels of their jackets. (*Author's collection*)

Previous page, below: A *c.* 1900 playing card that was part of a set made by the United States Playing Card Co. and published by The Waters Co. featuring early photographs of Washington, D.C., landmarks. Each card front features an image of the *Statue of Freedom*, also known as *Armed Freedom* or simply *Freedom*, the bronze statue that has crowned the dome of the U.S. Capitol building in Washington, D.C., since 1863. Originally named *Freedom Triumphant in War and Peace*, the statue depicts a female figure wearing a military helmet and holding a sheathed sword in her right hand with a laurel wreath and shield in her left. The statue's origin, dating from Lincoln's time, makes the inclusion of the house where Lincoln died all the more poignant. The image of the statue can be found in the center of the ace of spades of many decks of cards to the present day. (*Author's collection*)

Above left: An "Imperial" sized Cabinet Card photograph (9.75 by 6.75 inches) dating from around 1900. This particular photo, from Boyoe Studio at 1325 F Street NW, a short two-minute walk from Oldroyd's museum, was apparently commissioned by Col. Oldroyd for sale to guests visiting his museum. The image supports an urban legend circulating around the HWLD during Oldroyd's tenure there by virtue of the placement of the American flag in a second floor window instead of its usual position on the uppermost floor. Lincoln authority and author Dr. J. T. Hobbs details the legend in his book *Footprints of Abraham Lincoln* (Dayton, Ohio: The Otterbein Press, 1909) by saying, "In some pictures of the house in which Lincoln died there is a flag floating from a window in the second story, and in others the third story, with the statement that the flag indicates the room in which President Lincoln died. Neither is correct. He died in a small room on the first floor, in the rear part of the building." The building's original slate roof, visible in this image, was replaced with tin roofing in 1914 (like the building south of the HWLD at 514). (*Author's collection*)

Above right: In 1901, Curator Oldroyd published *The Assassination of Abraham Lincoln. Flight, Pursuit, Capture, and Punishment of the Conspirators*, a 305-page narrative account of Lincoln's death that became an instant bestseller. The closing chapter of the book is titled, "Narrative of a Walk of the Author, May, 1901, Over the Route of Flight and Capture." Oldroyd began his walk from the front door of the HWLD at 4 a.m. on Sunday May 12, 1901. For the 80-mile journey, Oldroyd carried with him a brand-new $2 Kodak No. 2 Brownie camera, which came preloaded with a 100-exposure roll of film. When the roll was finished, the entire machine was sent back to the factory in Rochester, NY, for developing. These earliest Kodak photographs were printed in a circular format small enough to be held in the palm of the hand. Oldroyd's walk is viewed as an evidentiary gold mine by modern day historians and features some of the earliest photographic images of homes and landmarks along Booth's escape route. This photo is the first of that series and represents what the HWLD looked at the turn-of-the-century. (*Photo courtesy National Park Service Ford's Theatre Historic Site archives*)

Above left: A *c.* 1901 postcard of the HWLD revealing (for the first time) the English basement office of Dr. Benjamin Tiefenthaler in the form of a "shingle" sign to the right of the door. On April 23, 1895, twenty-year-old Daisy Oldroyd married Dr. Benjamin Francis Tiefenthaler in the house where Lincoln died. The young couple moved to Cleveland, but within a short time, the newlyweds were back in the district, residing with their in-laws. Osborn and Lida's only grandchild, Josephine Oldroyd Tiefenthaler, was born in the Petersen House on July 17, 1896. Dr. Tiefenthaler's office can be found listed in the 1903 city directory at 516 10th St. NW where he is listed as an "Allopath," a doctor practicing science-based, modern medicine. This postcard also shows the updated sign for the "Oldroyd Lincoln Memorial Collection" now touting over 3,000 items. Charles Rousseau's marble marker, a fixture on the HWLD since August of 1879, has disappeared leaving only a faint shadow. Whether the sign crumbled from years of exposure or was removed by Osborn Oldroyd is unknown and soon evidence of its former prominence could only be found in old photos and postcards. (*Author's collection*)

Above right: This view of the house where Lincoln died shows the museum as it looked in 1902. Captured in this photograph is six-year-old Josephine Oldroyd Tiefenthaler playing on the stoop near the door of her father's doctor's office. The little girl, a familiar sight to visitors to the home, was fond of reciting patriotic poems for interested guests to the museem. She was the constant companion of her beloved grandfather, Osborn H. Oldroyd. The photo features the prominent sign that reads: "The House in Which Abraham Lincoln Died Contains the Oldroyd Lincoln Memorial Collection of over 3,000 Articles. Open At All Hours. Admission 25 Cents." The business next door at 518 10th St. NW is the "Yale Steam Laundry." Schade's newspaper sign, removed almost a decade before, can be detected by the large rectangular area of discoloration above the girl. (*Library of Congress*)

Next page, above: This image, dated 1909, represents a stereo-view photograph (also known as a stereoscopic photograph, stereograph, or, simply, a view) depicting the HWLD in a unique double image. Stereoscopic images are taken with a special camera fitted with two lenses spaced beside each other. It produces two nearly-identical images, each taken a few inches apart, offering a central image with minute differences. When viewed through two lenses of a stereoscope set 2.5 inches apart (approximately the space between the eyes) the result presents the illusion of a three-dimensional image. Because the stereoscope preceded the publication of photographs in newspapers and magazines, stereo viewers offered the first form of 3D entertainment for the masses. The building at 518 10th St. NW is for lease and Oldroyd's sign announcing that "This House is Open All Hours" is visible to the left of the larger descriptive marker affixed to the front railing. This view is particularly interesting because it represents the past meeting the future by featuring two horse-drawn vehicles (one pulled by a horse with blinders on) alongside an early motor car. (*Author's collection*)

A pair of images of Lincoln museum curator Osborn H. Oldroyd (1842–1930). The image at left, *c.* 1900, pictures Oldroyd in his typical daily curator's outfit consisting of a single-breasted jacket and polka-dotted ascot/cravat-style necktie. He sports the early version round lapel pin bearing the seal of the Grand Army of the Republic on his left jacket lapel. The image at right dates from around 1926 and pictures Oldroyd, the veteran curator, wearing the approved G.A.R. uniform consisting of a dark blue double-breasted coat with a double row of bronze G.A.R. buttons. The same round lapel pin, seen in the earlier photo, adorns his jacket per regulation. His uniform is augmented by two more ornate Grand Army of the Republic badges, one featuring the "National Level, Past Officer" designation. The official G.A.R. membership badge, in the shape of a bronze star depicting a soldier and sailor clasping hands in front of a figure of liberty, hung from a small silk American flag ribbon with thirteen stars in the upper left blue field. Col. Oldroyd served as assistant adjutant general of the Department of Potomac, Grand Army of the Republic, for nearly three decades, spanning almost his entire career as HWLD museum director from 1893 to 1926. (*Author's collection*)

Above: A 4-inch wide by 3¼-inch tall "Magic Lantern" slide of the house where Lincoln died and the Oldroyd Museum from before World War I. These glass slides, once placed into a projecting device and lit up by lantern or candle light, projected a larger image on to a blank wall. The resulting projections were often used as animation for educational talks as a precursor to the PowerPoint presentations so familiar to us now. These magic lantern slideshows fascinated audiences living in a time before mainstream photography and motion pictures. Oldroyd, a voracious walker who routinely walked for hundreds of miles at a stretch, used slides like this to augment his travel lectures and promote his museum. (*Author's collection*)

Previous page, below: A pair of *c.* 1900–1910s postcard views picturing the house where Lincoln died with the American flag flying from the northern most window of the building's top floor. These represent an early example of "photo-shopping" an image. The black and white postcard at left pictures curator Osborn Oldroyd and his wife, Lida, chatting in front of the door to the English basement. The building at right features a large business relocation sign in the window and another man and woman standing in the opposite doorway. The photo at right has been hand colored, the sign in the window of the adjoining building removed, and the man and woman cropped out of the picture. Notice that curtains have been added to the windows and the American flag flies from a different window than in previous views of the HWLD. Also missing from the building next door is the distinctive balcony and wrought iron railing seen in earlier views. (*Author's collection*)

Above left: This image, dating from around 1907, pictures two day laborers walking purposefully past the HWLD and the adjoining "Yale Steam Laundry" at 518 10th St. NW. One, wearing a leather apron and newsboy cap, carries his stein-shaped lunch pail in his hand while another man, wearing a fashionable straw skimmer hat and shirtsleeve garters, carries a small oil lantern in his hand. During this era, factory workers filled the pails with their lunch and, when finished, sent a boy off to the saloon to fill them with beer as water was often non-potable and not approved by appropriate authorities as being safe for consumption. A cyclist can be seen just entering the frame at right and Dr. B. F. Tiefenthaler's "shingle" sign can be seen affixed to the western-facing wall of the HWLD's English basement. Once again, the shadow of Louis Schade's newspaper sign is visible, but soon the last shades of Schade would disappear forever. (*Author's collection*)

Above right: A postcard from 1908 picturing the curator, wearing a stylish straw skimmer hat, posed on the front steps of his museum. The American flag can be seen partially furled in the southern most window of the third floor. This uppermost section of the building was used as the living quarters of the family that consisted of Colonel Osborn H. Oldroyd, his wife, Lida, their daughter, Daisy, her husband, Dr. Benjamin Francis Tiefenthaler, and granddaughter, Josephine. As with all comparable houses from this period, the building's upper floors follow a similar configuration but the ceiling height and window pane height decrease from the first to the third floors. This view is unique because it shows a wooden "Gingerbread" screen door and a retractable candy cane-striped awning above the entrance. Each window contains a woven wire mesh window screen in an adjustable wooden frame. The flag hangs from a 16-foot-long hand-turned mahogany flagpole nesting in a cast bronze cannon tube mount, supported by a pair of telescoping rods to secure it to the building. From this time on, the flag's positioning did not change. (*Author's collection*)

Above left: This postcard, from before World War I, offers a view of the distinctive stairs and entrance to the HWLD looking southeast down 10th Street. The awning and screen door are still in place along with an additional sign attached to the northern side of the porch railing designed to attract the attention of streetcars and automobile traffic traveling towards the White House on busy Pennsylvania Avenue. The large lettered sign reads: "House in Which Abraham Lincoln Died" and could be seen a block and a half away. From 1898 to 1917, the house had been under the jurisdiction of the war department, with Colonel Theodore A. Bingham of the U.S. Army Corps of Engineers as the officer in charge. From 1917 to 1933, the HWLD was under the auspices of the director of Public Buildings and Public Parks of the National Capital. (*Author's collection*)

Above right: The HWLD, again looking southeast across 10th Street, as it appeared around 1919. The awning and the screen door have been removed and a Lincoln-themed candy store now occupies the sales space next door. The "Abe Lincoln Candies" company made candies of all types, sizes, and flavors, which they shipped all over the East Coast. According to the July 1920 *Confectioners Journal* trade magazine (p. 130), the brand was sold to William A. Esterday for $10,000 and relocated to Baltimore and Silver Spring, Maryland. At the time, the adjoining building at 518 10th St. NW also housed the "Alfred A. Ray Electrical Blue Printer" company and another business known simply as "Dad's Place." (*Library of Congress*)

Above left: This image appeared on p. 29 of the *Washington Evening Star* newspaper of Friday April 8, 1921 in a column called "Travelog Boy" by Russell Burke. The caption reads (in part): "Dear boys and girls.... Just around the corner in 10th St., from busy F St., is the house where Lincoln died. I have received many letters asking me about the house, so I went to see it again the other day.... The house is the one to which the President was carried. It has the old-fashioned steps leading up to the front door with the turn in them that was so customary in houses during the Civil War days. There is also an entrance right off the street and under the little platform at the top of the stairs that go to the front door. Thousands of people have visited this little house since that Good Friday in April nearly 60 years ago. There are many interesting things to be seen there, and I looked at the hand writing of the great President, both when a boy and when he became President. The collection is called the Col. O. H. Oldroyd collection, for he spent years in getting together data and things connected with Lincoln. There is Lincoln's favorite rocking chair, a rail he split in 1830—just think, that is ninety-one years ago—and a stand made of logs from a house in Illinois where Lincoln once lived. There is a handbill telling how the War Department offered $100,000 for the capture of Booth, and you can see the spur Booth wore. This is the one that caught in the curtain of the President's box and caused Booth's leg to break in falling to the stage." (*Author's collection*)

Above right: This image depicts a young lady dressed in classic 1920s "Flapper Girl" style. She is attired in a stylish Georgette dress accented by black cuffs and a collared single button shoulder frock. Her look is topped by a Gatsby-style bell-shaped Cloche hat with a large bow in the back that undoubtedly hides her pageboy haircut. This image offers a close-up view of the awning shading the door behind her. Judging by its height, the awning had a short life at the HWLD as no doubt many visitors lost their hats or bumped their heads on it while entering the museum. (*Author's collection*)

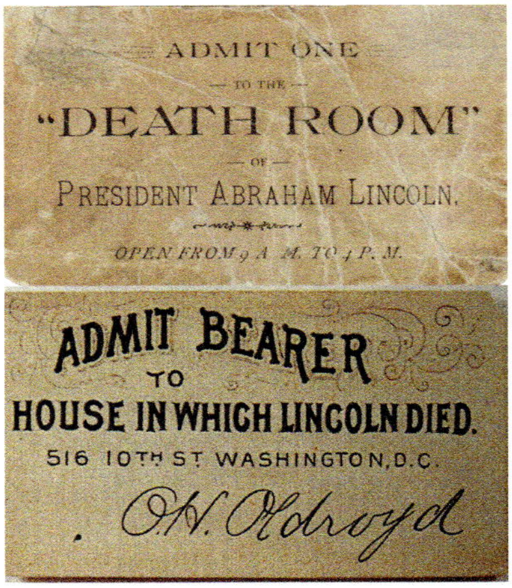

Left: Examples of two tickets for admission to the Oldroyd Museum inside the house where Lincoln died. The upper ticket dates from before World War I and the lower ticket is from the post-World War I era. Although Oldroyd kept a register in the front hallway for his guests to sign in on, they were incomplete and limited mostly to noteworthy visitors and guests from other states, therefore accurate attendance figures are impossible to calculate. However, that number would certainly run into the hundreds of thousands during his three decades in Washington, D.C. (*Author's collection*)

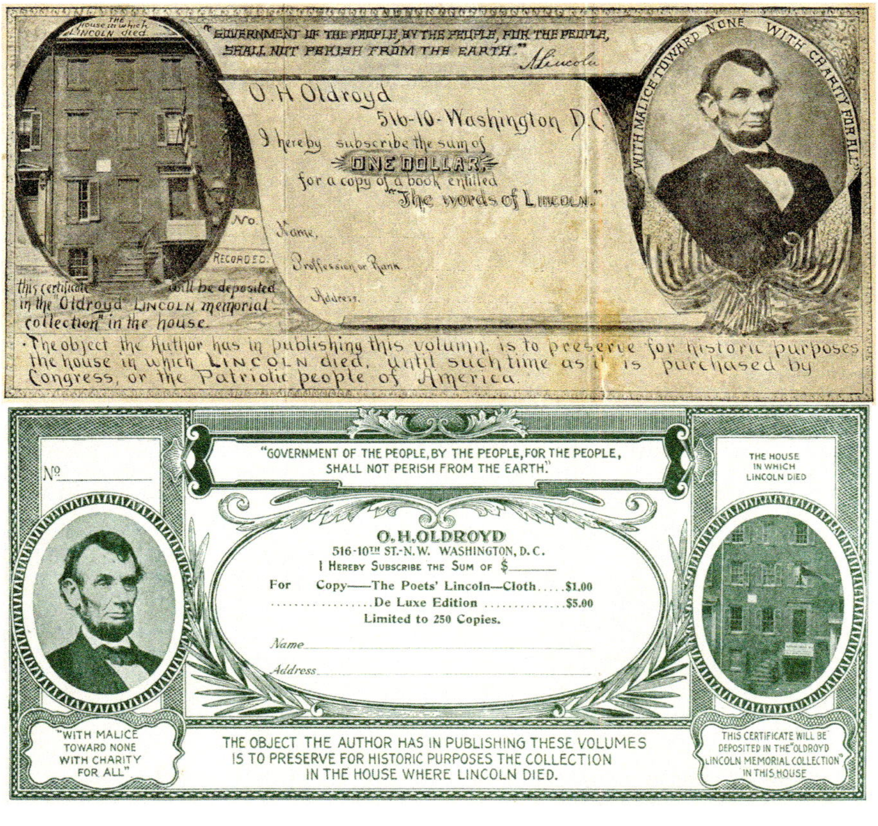

A pair of specially printed donor's certificates, each measuring 8¼ inches wide by 4 inches tall, were created by curator Oldroyd and used as receipts for contributions of $1 by visitors to the museum. The upper photo, dating from before the World War I era, offers a copy of Oldroyd's 1895 book *Words of Lincoln* as a donor gift. The lower image, post-World War I, was created as a donor's receipt for the purchase of Oldroyd's 1915 book *The Poet's Lincoln*. Each individually numbered certificate contained a spot for the recipient's name and address making it, along with Oldroyd's guest register, a very effective method of populating a mailing list for future sales. (*Author's collection*)

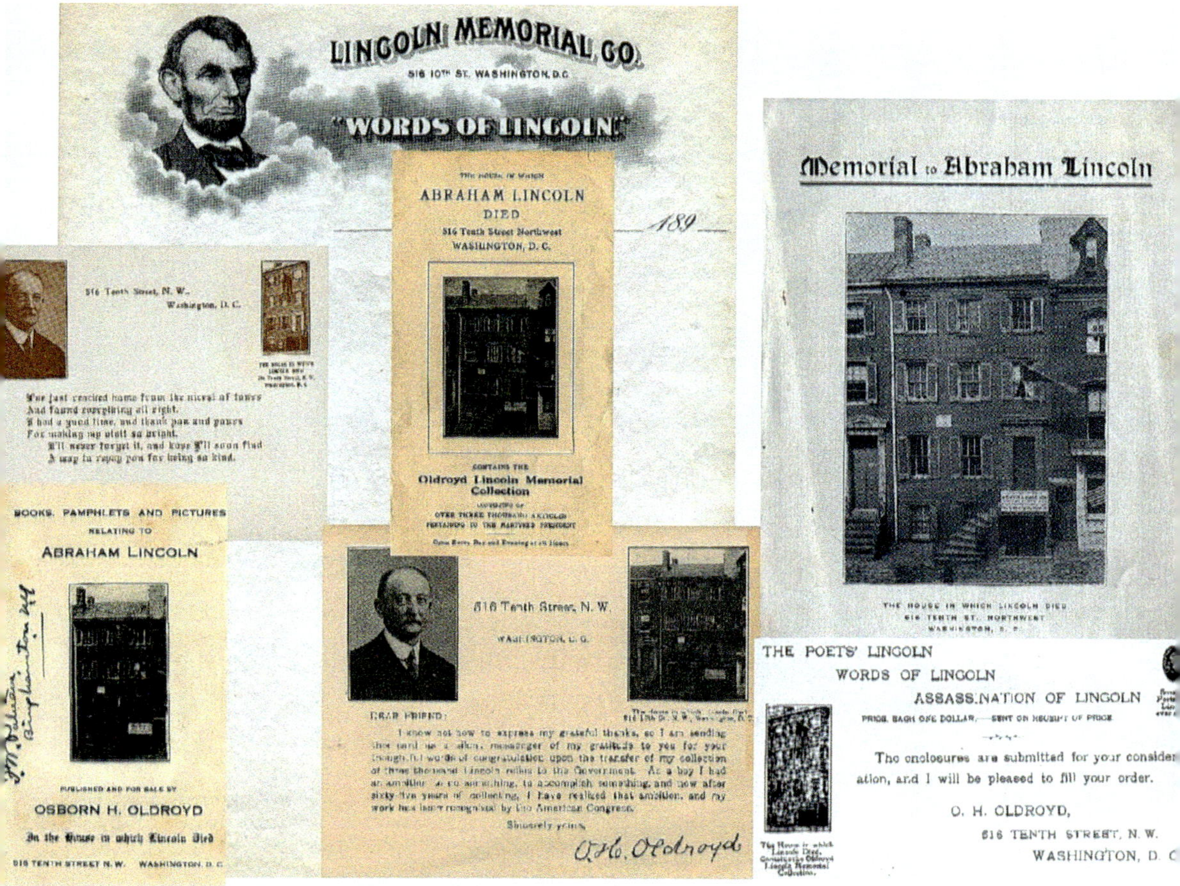

A selection of eight different brochures and mailers generated by Col. Oldroyd to promote his Lincoln museum in the HWLD from the 1890s to the 1920s. These type of handouts and direct mail circulars, along with his seven books and many pamphlets written during the same era, represent some of the earliest forms of direct contact advertising campaigns. Oldroyd's brochures offer testimonials about the museum or the curator himself and highlight an ever changing list of items on display from his collection that varied from 2,500 to 3,000 items over that period. During his thirty years in the HWLD, Oldroyd's museum displayed the rocking chair in which the president died, the top hat the president was wearing, and the Treasury flag that adorned the box at Ford's Theatre, all of which were ultimately removed and placed in other institutions and all of which are considered priceless relics of the Lincoln tragedy today. (*Author's collection*)

Oldroyd's 1908 booklet *The Centenary of the Birth of Abraham Lincoln 1809–1909. Program of Exercises in Commemoration of that Event* proved so popular that nine known editions exist. Of this work, *The National Tribune* of November 5, 1908 (p. 8) said: "Capt. Oldroyd keeps every scrap of print which has Lincoln's name in it; every picture that is printed, painted or etched of him; every opinion that has been expressed of him; in fact, he lets nothing escape that bears in any way upon the life of Lincoln.... He has become famous the world over. He has made a study of Lincoln's life, and so no one is better fitted to put out a tentative program for observance of Lincoln's birthday. It was Captain Oldroyd's idea that all over the country at about the same hour the Grand Army of the Republic and its allied societies, as well as the other patriotic and civic societies, might be meeting to do honor to the name of America's greatest President, and that around the land on that day and hour a great electric flash of patriotism would illuminate the country." The pamphlet on the right details his career as a "pedestrian" and, in particular, his 1907 lecture detailing his walk through Ireland, Scotland, Wales, and England—a trip of over 1,200 miles. He visited over 100 points of interest along the way and he did it all on foot. His lecture, "illustrated" by the use of magic lantern slides, was a popular fundraiser for the G.A.R. veterans post in the District. (*Author's collection*)

Next page, above: A magic lantern slide from the pre-World War I era picturing the room where Abraham Lincoln died as it appeared while Oldroyd was displaying his collection there. This image, looking west, represents the distortion that exists between one of these light-sensitive lantern glass slides and a photograph. Although the image appears darkened and distorted to the naked eye, once illuminated, it popped and fairly glowed to reveal details hidden in the darkness. Photographic lantern slides reached the peak of their popularity during the first third of the twentieth century, and dramatically impacted the development of animation technologies and visual-based education methods in all fields. Within a generation after this slide was produced, magic lantern shows became a rarity and ultimately obsolete. (*Author's collection*)

Below: A photographic image of the same scene represented above. Abraham Lincoln's bench, which once adorned the back porch of the Springfield home, can be seen in the foreground. Mr. Lincoln had a local carpenter, Solomon Conant, build the extra-long wooden settee bench as a place to stretch out after a long work day. A pair of Lincoln family chairs rest nearby while on the opposite wall an 1860 Lincoln and Hamlin campaign flag hangs below the eagle that once adorned the Lincoln catafalque that traveled from Washington to Springfield. The cases seen in this image are filled with a dizzying assortment of Lincoln funeral relics. Oldroyd was considered to have the first complete collection of photographs of the conspirators and relics from the assassination, which drew a near constant stream of researchers to his museum. Additionally, this image offers a good view of the extension added by the curator after he removed the rear wall of the death room to facilitate extra exhibit space. (*Author's collection*)

A photograph of the room in which Abraham Lincoln died as seen from the rear doorway of Oldroyd's added exhibit space and facing east towards the entrance of the HWLD. The walls are adorned with paintings, prints and newspapers from Oldroyd's collection and the "x" scrawled next to the chair delineates the spot where the bed stood that night. The original bed frame and mattresses were sold by the Petersen family for $80 at auction in late 1871. For years, an effort was made to bring the bed, purchased by Chicago candy magnate Charles Gunther, back to this hallowed spot but it never materialized. Instead, the Lincoln deathbed was placed on display at the Chicago Historical Society where it remains today. (*Author's collection*)

A photograph of the Oldroyd museum looking west and picturing the space between the adjoining front and rear parlors, both of which are stuffed full of Lincoln relics. The parlors are mirror images of each other, measuring 14½ feet by 16½ feet each, and when the doors are opened, it creates the effect of one large room. In the foreground is the front parlor where Reverend Phineas D. Gurley prayed with First Lady Mary Lincoln as her husband lay dying down the long hall. Behind the archway, the back parlor is accentuated by the marble-top center table, a reminder that it was here that Secretary of War Edwin M. Stanton, between visits to the death room across the hall, took notes as he questioned witnesses concerning the tragic shooting of the president. Oldroyd has stacked the central table in the foreground with free brochures and penny postcards, which he encouraged his visitors to send back home to friends and loved ones. (*Author's collection*)

A photograph of a typical display in one of the parlors of Oldroyd's Lincoln Museum. Objects visible in this photo include a photograph of Lincoln's hat, which was once displayed in the museum until a famous court case returned it the Smithsonian; John Wilkes Booth's spur, which caught on the flag adorning the theatre box; a pair of brackets that formerly adorned the presidential box at the time of the assassination; and dozens of autographs, photographs, and memorabilia of Lincoln and the murderous conspirators. Over the years, as seen in this photo, the cluttered condition of the Oldroyd collection caused concern for threat of fire resulting in its eventual purchase and relocation to Ford's Theatre by the Federal Government. The first fire detection/alarm systems at the HWLD were not installed until 1937 (and updated in 1949, 1951, and 1978). (*Author's collection*)

This photo, dated February 10, 1922 by the National Photo Co. of Washington D.C., is captioned: "Theo Hardy, famous actor now living in Washington D.C. photographed in the role of Abraham Lincoln at the house on 10th St. in which the martyred President died." The photo is important as it shows the wooden sign displayed between the first and second floor behind the railing of the HWLD. Placed there by the district's Committee on Marking Points of Interest, it features a red, white, and blue shield-shaped marker with the number 45 inset and reads: "In This House president Lincoln died April 15, 1865. Now contains the Oldroyd Lincoln Memorial collection." Made of painted wood, these signs were ill-equipped to endure the seasonal rain, sleet, and snow of the city and did not last long. (*Author's collection*)

Above left: This image of the HWLD dates from around 1924 and offers a view of the museum and neighboring businesses during the Roaring Twenties in the district. The building immediately south of the HWLD, at 514, is a six-story commercial structure known as the "Lincoln Building" that was constructed in 1923 after the original 1849 three-and-a-half-story row house was demolished. The building immediately north, at 518, is a four-story mixed-use building constructed in 1873 that replaced the original row house that was there in 1865. No. 518 housed the "Lincoln Cafe," which offered bistro-style seating during the day and cocktails at night. Bicycles lean against the lamppost and a 1924 Ford Model T Fordor sedan automobile is parked on the street out front of the iconic curved sandstone stairway. The window and entryway awnings are still in place at the HWLD and the cafe has added a retractable awning above the tables and chairs located yards away from the museum's doorway. Also visible in this image is the new tin roof on the HWLD, added after 1914. (*Photo courtesy National Park Service Ford's Theatre Historic Site archives*)

Above right: This photo of the HWLD stands out because the photographer has captured the brief period when the Oldroyd Museum was between signs. Dating from the period before World War I, the original sign featured a white background and read: "This House In Which Abraham Lincoln, Died, Contains 2500 Relics Relating To The Martyred President, Most Of Them From His Homestead At Springfield, Illinois" with specific hours and days of operation listed. It was replaced by a sign with a black background and a beveled picture frame edge that read: "House in Which Abraham Lincoln Died Contains the Oldroyd Memorial Collection of Over 3000 Articles. Open At All Hours." Osborn Oldroyd had left Springfield far behind him, his collection had grown vastly, and his museum was now firmly entrenched in the nation's capital. (*Photo courtesy National Park Service Ford's Theatre Historic Site archives*)

The change of signs from white to black did not last long though. In this undated image, a small child wearing a floppy straw hat can be seen resting on the iconic steps leading up to the entrance of the HWLD. The ever-present flag has yet to be unfurled, a bicycle (presumably belonging to the photographer) rests against the railing as a man stares back at the camera through the open second-story window of the business next door. The streetlight seen in previous photos has disappeared, replaced by a fire hydrant. A new, larger awning covers half the door and the sign reveals that the admission price has changed to 30 cents by the addition of a local tax. Oldroyd, a lifelong Republican, is obviously countering the many "Revenue Acts" of the 1920s enacted under Secretary of the Treasury Andrew Mellon who served three Republican presidents from 1920 to 1932. Although, as the sign states, the tax rate was 2 cents, Oldroyd has added an additional 3-cent increase of his own, mirroring the prosperity of the Roaring Twenties. (*Photo courtesy National Park Service Ford's Theatre Historic Site archives*)

A stereo-view image of the HWLD from the 1920s era. It remains important because it reveals that, like the entryway, the windows of the Oldroyd family living quarters on the HWLD's upper floors were also shaded by striped awnings. The streetlight has been replaced near the fire hydrant. The photo represents one of the last views of the distinctive 10-foot-tall brick chimney on the south side of the roof, which would soon be truncated to a height of 2 feet. The building next door at 518 10th NW is now occupied by Chas. E. Kritch's leather goods shop at street level and the offices of the "Alfred A. Ray Electrical Blue Printer" company are housed in the upper levels. (*Author's collection*)

Above left: This photograph was taken on February 12, 1918 during Abraham Lincoln's birthday celebration in the district. It remains unique in that it is one of the few images surviving that depicts the HWLD with snow on the ground. Interest always ramped up during February around Lincoln's birthday, and although Oldroyd's critics accused the curator of P. T. Barnum-style profiteering by charging 2 bits admission to his museum, it should be noted that Oldroyd was not all about the money. The March 4, 1909 edition of the *National Tribune* reported: "On Lincoln's birthday and during the week before Capt. Oldroyd always throws his house open for school children to inspect the relics. Some 10,000 of the school children of Washington, under care of their several teachers, tramped through the historic rooms during the free days last month. It was an object lesson to all of them." (*Author's collection*)

Above right: This image dates from the 1920s era and offers an excellent view of the stairs and entryway to the HWLD with a makeshift "hot-dip" galvanized metal awning housing attached to the former wrought iron balcony of the building next door. A pair of distinctive looking women are posed rather sternly at the top step next to a young man whose hand is holding back the awning at 518 as it flaps in the wind. The image offers a close-up view of the iron railing and reveals that each stair railing picket (or baluster) contains a single knuckle in the center for added tensile strength. The photo is equally important as it offers a closer view of the HWLD admission sign confirming the price increase of 30 cents. (*Photo courtesy National Park Service Ford's Theatre Historic Site archives*)

This 1920s era Kodak snapshot photo pictures an unidentified young couple standing at the top of the stairs of the HWLD. The older, well-dressed gentleman is veteran curator Osborn H. Oldroyd posed proudly on the sidewalk near the fire hydrant. By now, Oldroyd was an accomplished author, world traveler, respected G.A.R. officer, and recognized expert on Abraham Lincoln. At the time of this photo, Oldroyd had witnessed the passing of Lida's parents (the Stonebergers), his son-in-law, Dr. Benjamin Tiefenthaler, and his only granddaughter, Josephine, in the HWLD. These sad passings are important to the house's story because they illustrate that although it was an important historic landmark, it was also a home. From an obvious historic standpoint, while Lincoln was the most noteworthy death in the building, the Petersen and Oldroyd families lost loved ones here too. (*Photo courtesy National Park Service Ford's Theatre Historic Site archives*)

During Osborn H. Oldroyd's stewardship of the HWLD there were many changes and improvements made to the property. On March 3, 1899 Congress appropriated $3,833.50 for the first set of repairs on the house in work completed on June 30, 1900. By July 8, 1899, a two-story rear wing addition including a coal shed and a storeroom were completed. Other improvements, all supervised by the Army Corps of Engineers, included another room added to the rear of the second story, new plumbing installed, and gas pipes and fixtures updated and repaired. In 1908, the first floor level back porch was enclosed by a wooden and glass partition. In 1914, the original slate roof was replaced with one made of galvanized tin, and in 1922, a new steam boiler was installed. This postcard, issued a few years before Oldroyd's collection was purchased by the U.S. Government in 1926, offers a view of the obtrusive green and white candy cane-striped awning over the doorway that, although it matches the green window shutters, did little to assuage the resonant solemnity of the building's history. (*Author's collection*)

Above: On April 29, 1924, in ceremonies presided over by Congressman-at-large Henry R. Rathbone, Jr., two plaques were unveiled: one on Ford's Theatre (pictured here) and the other on the house where Lincoln died. Henry Riggs Rathbone was the son of Maj. Henry R. and Clara (Harris) Rathbone who were guests in the box at Ford's theatre on the evening the president was shot. Three of the four iconic arched doorways of the theatre have been partially bricked up and turned into windows. A military band is seated at rest to the right of the speaker and Allen C. Clark, president of the Columbia Historical Society from 1916 until his death in 1943, is seated behind Congressman Rathbone. The plaque affixed that day to Ford's Theatre has since disappeared while the plaque unveiled that same day remains firmly attached to the HWLD. (*Photo courtesy National Park Service Ford's Theatre Historic Site archives*)

Below: Mrs. Osborn H. Oldroyd (Lida) drew the drapery cord to unveil the tablet on the house where Lincoln died. The plaque, unveiled in 1924 and still attached to the HWLD today, reads: "Abraham Lincoln Died In This House April 15, 1865 at 7:22 A.M. Purchased By The United States in 1896." In early 1924, Representative Rathbone, a Republican of Chicago, Illinois, sponsored a bill in Congress to purchase the Oldroyd collection for $ 50,000 for permanent display in the HWLD. At the time, Oldroyd had been displaying his collection of Lincoln relics in the Petersen House for thirty years. (*Photo by Rhonda S. Hunter*)

Oldroyd was growing old and by the time this photo was taken in the spring of 1924, he had been collecting Lincoln objects for over sixty years. Rathbone's bill was simply the latest of many such articles introduced by politicians over the past few decades. Oldroyd was hedging his bets by proposing to move the collection back to its original location in Springfield, Illinois, should Rathbone's bill fail. This Rotogravure photo by Harris & Ewing, taken in front of one of Oldroyd's museum displays during that time, was captioned: "Famous collection of relics, owned by Capt. O.H. Oldroyd (left), and housed in the little brick structure on 10th Street, Washington, where the Emancipator died, may be moved to Illinois unless Congress votes to buy it this session. Representative Rathbone of Illinois, (right) has asked Congress to purchase it." (*Photo courtesy Lincoln Financial Collection Allen County Library, Fort Wayne, Indiana*)

On May 11, 1926, by act of Congress, the U.S. Government became the owner of the Osborn Oldroyd collection of Lincoln relics. This Rotogravure photo by Harris & Ewing, was headlined "UNCLE SAM BUYS LINCOLN RELICS" and was captioned: "Part of the famous Oldroyd Collection in a corner of the old house on 10th Street in Washington where Lincoln died the day after he was shot in Ford's Theatre. Capt. O.H. Oldroyd (left), former owner of the relics, is shown with Representative H.L. Rathbone (sic) of Illinois, to whose efforts is due the government purchase for $ 50,000. Henry Ford and others had sought to buy the collection." The duo are pictured in front of a display case crowded with relics of the assassination including photos of the conspirators, Booth's erstwhile spur, and the key of the prison in which the conspirators were incarcerated. (*Photo courtesy Lincoln Financial Collection Allen County Library, Fort Wayne, Indiana*)

This photo from the ACME news agency is dated March 18, 1926. It pictures Curator Oldroyd alongside Ohio Senator Frank Willis, an oft-forgotten figure in the Oldroyd saga who also deserves credit for shepherding the purchase and preservation of the Oldroyd collection through the U.S. Senate in 1926. Franklin Bartlett Willis (1871–1928) was an Ohio Republican who served as congressman (1900–1915), then governor (1915–1917), and finally as U.S. senator (replacing Warren G. Harding) from 1921 until his death in 1928. The photo is captioned: "O. H. Oldroyd, right, has devoted the last 69 years to assembling and collecting the mementos of Abraham Lincoln. They are all housed in the old building on 10th St., Washington, D.C, where Lincoln died. If the government does not buy this collection it will be sold to private buyers and removed from Washington. Henry Ford has made a large bid for the collection. World's greatest collection of Lincoln relics." (*Author's collection*)

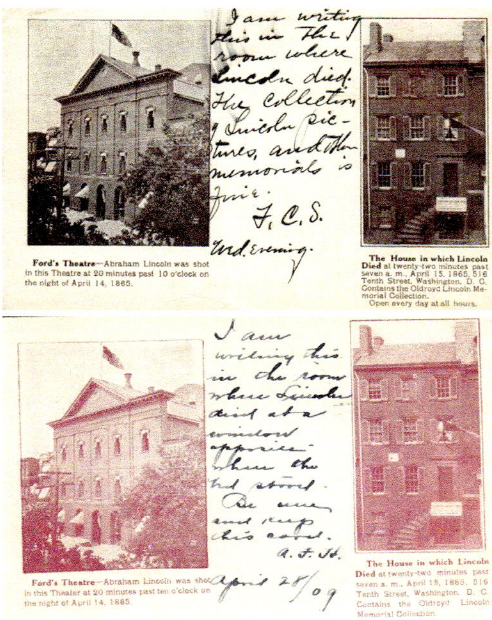

Here are two typical penny postcards which Oldroyd sold and encouraged his visitors to send back home to friends and loved ones. The postcards featured an image of Ford's Theatre (left) and the HWLD (right). One, mailed to Addison, Maine, in 1911, reads "I am writing this in the room where Lincoln died. The collection of Lincoln pictures and other memorials is fine. F. C.S. Wed. Evening" while the other, mailed to Arlington, Massachusetts, reads: "I am writing this in the room where Lincoln died at a window opposite where the bed stood. Be sure and keep this card. A.F.H. April 28, 1909." The curator often advised visitors to write these postcards while seated in the chairs or at the desk of President Lincoln inside his museum for an extra-special experience. (*Author's collection*)

Above: This photo from early September of 1926 pictures Rep. Rathbone (left) and Oldroyd (right) in the HWLD. Rathbone is presenting a copy of the House Bill he sponsored to Oldroyd who is holding the pen that President Calvin Coolidge used to sign the bill into law on August 30. Oldroyd's collaboration with Congressman Rathbone was indeed a propitious one. Rathbone was an Illinois lawyer who served only five years in Congress, but luckily for Captain Oldroyd, those five years coincided with his final push to sell his Lincoln collection. Spearheading the purchase of Oldroyd's Lincoln collection and leading the charge to have Ford's Theatre and the house where Lincoln died properly marked as landmarks were the capstones of Rathbone's Congressional career. (*Photo courtesy National Park Service Ford's Theatre Historic Site archives*)

Below: This image, taken sometime in the fall of 1926, features Oldroyd's champion, Henry Riggs Rathbone, posed standing on the sidewalk in front of the distinctive curved iron railing leading up to Oldroyd's museum. When the photo is examined more closely, the figure of a man can be seen peeking out of the front parlor window over Rathbone's right shoulder. That man is Osborn H. Oldroyd perpetrating what surely must be one of the earliest photo bombs in the history of photography. Rathbone—sometimes called "Harry" and sometimes "Riggs"—had been born on Lincoln's birthday, February 12, 1870. Rathbone died on July 15, 1928 in Chicago, fifty-seven years to the day that Lincoln's son, Tad, died on July 15, 1871. (*Photo courtesy National Park Service Ford's Theatre Historic Site archives*)

Above: This photo pictures Oldroyd seated at his desk at the moment of triumph after selling his collection to the U.S. on July 30, 1926. Oldroyd is seated in front of his massive roll top desk, its innumerable compartments stuffed full with letters, documents, and assorted correspondence. In his hands rest the neatly framed object that started it all over six decades before, the original Abraham Lincoln pulp paper booklet a teenaged Oldroyd found back in Mt. Vernon, Ohio. The captain kept the frame hanging above his desk, pointed it out to every museum visitor, and consulted it quite often. Look closely over Oldroyd's left shoulder and you will see a framed picture of a little girl holding chocolate-covered ice cream bars, one in each hand. That little girl is Josephine (Oldroyd) Tiefenthaler, Osborn and Lida's only grandchild who died in the HWLD on February 20, 1908. Ironically, her death came on the forty-sixth anniversary of Willie Lincoln's death at the White House, a sad story Osborn Oldroyd knew well. (*Author's collection*)

Below: This photo, dating from the mid-1920s, features an unidentified man posed in front of the HWLD. Although Oldroyd delighted in his role as historical tour guide, others occasionally helped lead tours through the museum during the curator's absence. His wife, Lida, daughter, Daisy, and young granddaughter, Josephine, all helped usher guests through the museum at times, but obviously this image is none of them. Osborn's brother-in-law, Benjamin Franklin Stoneberger, lived in the HWLD and assisted with tours and other chores, so this may well be him. It would fall to B. F. Stoneberger, along with his sister, Osborn's widow, Lida, to sort through the family's personal possessions contained in the HWLD after Oldroyd's death on October 9, 1930. Even more ironically, Stoneberger enjoyed a 40-year career in Chicago as an employee of the Chas. Gunther candy company, much of that time helping catalog and assess Gunther's Lincoln collection which included the bed in which Abraham Lincoln died. (*Library of Congress*)

Above: This photo from the summer of 1926 pictures HWLD curator Osborn H. Oldroyd standing on the spot where Lincoln died while pointing to a large framed artist's depiction of the death scene hanging on the wall. This larger print is surrounded by several other smaller framed depictions of Lincoln's final moments. There were many different versions of the death scene, some featuring as few as twelve witnesses, others as many as forty-seven crammed into this tiny 9½-foot-wide by 17-foot-long sleeping room whose slanted ceiling made it appear even smaller. Oldroyd stands near artist John Rogers' statue titled *Council of War*, which itself was created in three different versions. Equally important is the presence of the print known as *The Blacksmith's Apprentice*, which occupies the same spot on the wall as it did the night the president died. (*Author's collection*)

Below: This Columbia Broadcasting System photo, dated February 5, 1931, pictures Lewis Gardner Reynolds, the man who replaced Oldroyd as custodian at the HWLD standing in the precise spot as the photo above. Reynolds is delivering a radio address on the same spot where Oldroyd stood some five years previous. Reynolds's address, described by CBS as a "word-picture tour of the historic building," was broadcast on the 122nd anniversary of the birth of Abraham Lincoln. As part of his address, Reynolds declared: "No story of this Lincoln Relics Museum would be complete without special reference to Col. Osborn H. Oldroyd to whom the world is indebted for this collection. Col. Oldroyd spent 65 years in gathering together these intimate things. A monument should be erected to that man." (*Author's collection*)

Above left: This image ran in newspapers across the country on February 12, 1929 to coincide with Abraham Lincoln's 120th birthday. Titled *House Where Abraham Lincoln Died Shelters Aged Collectors of Lore*, it pictures curators Osborn H. Oldroyd, Lewis G. Reynolds, and Abraham Lincoln. The caption details how "each has dedicated his life to collecting mementos and documents of the Emancipator's life and work." Reynolds, who like his friend Oldroyd hailed originally from Ohio, became nationally known as the founder of carnation day, a tribute to assassinated President William McKinley. According to Reynolds, he had the distinction of being the last living person to encounter the living Lincoln. As a six-year-old child, he once sat upon Abraham Lincoln's knee. Mr. Reynolds delighted in sharing his story with guests and often handed out a pamphlet of his own, *A Wonderful Hour With Abraham Lincoln*, describing his encounter with the sixteenth president, which he often handed out to visitors to the museum. (*Photo courtesy Lincoln Financial Collection Allen County Library, Fort Wayne, Indiana*)

Above right: This 1926 rotogravure photo pictures Col. Osborn H. Oldroyd in front of a case of busts, medallions, and profile relief statues depicting Abraham Lincoln. During Oldroyd's three decades in Washington, D.C., he was famously approached by millionaire businessmen like J. P. Morgan and Henry Ford, both of whom wanted to purchase the collection. However, Oldroyd's dream was to sell his collection to the Federal government and, ultimately, retain it for the American people. His dream was realized when his collection was purchased by the Federal government. After the sale, Superintendent of Public Buildings and Public Parks Lt. Ulysses S Grant, III (1881–1968), grandson of President Grant, offered to let Oldroyd remain as Curator Emeritus of the museum, but Oldroyd declined, citing his advanced age. Upon hearing this, Col. Grant reached into his pocket and presented Oldroyd with the key to the Petersen House and invited him to come and go as he liked. The Oldroyd collection was placed on display in the basement of Ford's Theatre six years later and officially opened at 2 p.m. on February 12, 1932, the 123rd birthday of Abraham Lincoln. (*Author's collection*)

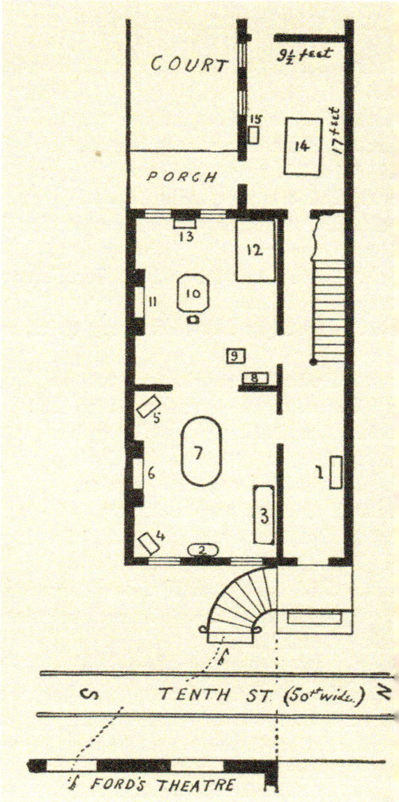

Above left: A collection of business cards from Lincoln museum curator Osborn H. Oldroyd created during his thirty-year tenure at the HWLD. Some pictured the historic building while others featured an image of the sixteenth president identified as the "Smallest Portrait of Lincoln ever made." Most list the 516 10th St. NW address, but two of them feature the curator's home address of 1723 Webster St. NW where the Oldroyd's moved after selling the collection. The card in the lower right-hand corner is that of Lewis Gardner Reynolds and it utilizes the same design as his predecessor. Aside from a short curatorial term by Captain John T. Clemens, Oldroyd and Reynolds were the sole curators of the Oldroyd collection while it was displayed in the HWLD. (*Author's collection*)

Above right: Diagram of the Oldroyd museum from p. 37 of the 1901 book *The Assassination of Abraham Lincoln. Flight, Pursuit, Capture, and Punishment of the Conspirators*. Some of the exhibits highlighted in Oldroyd's map include the "hat rack in the in hall" (1), "sofa, occupied by Mrs. Lincoln" (3), "fireplace" (6 and 11), "center table" (7), "washstand" (8), and "bed-not made up" (12). The curved stairs and entryway are easily identifiable and the Lincoln table (15) upon which Oldroyd encouraged his guests to write their postcards is seen across from Lincoln's death bed (14). Stanton's dispatch table, described earlier in this volume, is represented by number designation 10. (*Author's collection*)

Above: A collection of six different postcards picturing the HWLD died in the years after the collection moved across the street to Ford's Theatre. Dating from 1932 into the 1970s, they offer an assortment of signs denoting the building's historic significance. In 1932, under the leadership of Lt. Col. U.S. Grant, III, the first floor of the house was refurnished by five women's patriotic organizations and opened to the public. During this same timeframe, the Office of Public Buildings and Public Parks replaced the home's original gas fixtures with electric fixtures. On June 10, 1933, ownership of the HWLD was transferred to the National Park Service who undertook a major renovation from 1944 to 1945. The official bronze government marker can be seen in all of them but missing are Oldroyd's signs hawking a 25-cent admission fee. The signs now read simply, "House In Which Abraham Lincoln Died. Open Daily." (*Author's collection*)

Previous page, below: A pair of two postcard photos, on the left from the 1930s and on the right a contemporary view, that link the HWLD with Ford's Theatre. The pairing represents the only museums in Washington, D.C., solely dedicated to Abraham Lincoln. The Lincoln Monument on the National Mall, opened on May 30, 1922 in ceremonies that included the last public appearance of Robert Todd Lincoln, is a memorial, not a museum. Not only did the cross street move of Oldroyd's collection change location, it changed emphasis. The Ford's Theatre official blog aptly states "Only then would the site of the assassination, and not the site of Lincoln's death, become the center of the story." While Ford's Theatre has undergone extensive changes over the years, the HWLD remains largely intact. In fact, all of the "six-over-six, double-hung sash" windows in the HWLD are originals except for the northernmost one on the second floor.[7] (*Author's collection*)

Above left: The house where Lincoln died as it appeared in the 1970s era. The building next door displays a Coca-Cola "red disc" or "button" sign on the second floor. This view offers a good view of the large oval U.S. Government marker that replaced Oldroyd's garish signs hawking his museum. The sign features a stylized funerary laurel wreath with a mourning ribbon that reads: "United States Department of the Interior. National Park Service. House Where Lincoln Died. Hours: 9 A.M. To 5:00 P.M. Admission Free." This style sign is still in place to this day. (*Photo courtesy National Park Service Ford's Theatre Historic Site archives*)

Above right: This modern-day photo of the house where Lincoln died shows little change from images taken a half century previous. The National Park Service's intent for the HWLD falls within their purview of "Comprehensive Historic Preservation Planning," which they define as "the organization into a logical sequence of preservation information pertaining to identification, evaluation, registration, and treatment of historic properties, and setting priorities for accomplishing preservation activities." For this (and many other) properties, the NPS strives to maintain the "Integrity" of sites which they define as "the authenticity of a property's historic identity, evidenced by the survival of physical characteristics that existed during the property's historic or prehistoric period."[8] (*Photo by Rhonda S. Hunter*)

Above left: This photo, dated October 24, 1967, pictures a workman resting and smoking a cigar while perched on the sill of a second-story window at Ford's Theatre, looking across 10th Street at the house where Lincoln died. In 1964, Congress approved funds to restore Ford's Theatre to its 1865-era appearance. The restoration began in 1965 and continued for three years. On January 21, 1968 Ford's Theatre reopened as a national historic site and a working theatre. (*Author's collection*)

Above right: This photo, taken by the author on April 15, 2012 during a backstage tour of the Ford's Theatre on the 150th anniversary of the assassination, shows the modern view from the same window seen in the image above. The house where Lincoln died is dwarfed today by modern high-rise governmental office buildings. The neighborhood would be unrecognizable to the Petersen, Schade, and Oldroyd families who once called the building their home. According to the National Park Service, over 542,000 people, nearly 113,000 of whom were students, visited Ford's Theatre and the HWLD in 2019. The venue is now a working theatre and Oldroyd's collection has been incorporated into the state-of-the-art museum on its lower floor. The house where Lincoln died has been meticulously restored to its appearance of April 14, 1865 and remains one of the few surviving "snapshots in time" to be found in our nation's capital. (*Photo by Alan E. Hunter*)

Above: This stereo-view photo dates from 1892, the year before the Memorial Association of the District of Columbia purchased the HWLD and moved Osborn Oldroyd in. The image depicts the front and rear parlors during the time that Louis Schade and his family were still living in the home. The photo, taken by B. W. Kilburn, is captioned: "In this room the Cabinet, and Mrs. Lincoln awaited the event that Bowed Forty Millions of Hearts with Sorrow." It was in this double parlor that the search for the assassin was first planned. (*Photo courtesy National Park Service Ford's Theatre Historic Site archives*)

Below: This photo, part of the 1968 Historic American Buildings Survey (HABS), pictures the front and rear parlors recreated after the 1959 renovation of the HWLD to appear as it might have looked on the night of Lincoln's assassination. On that night, these rooms were the living quarters of George Francis, a furniture dealer whose store was located nearby at 490 Seventh Street, and his wife, Huddah. The renters were preparing for bed when news that the president had been shot was first heard on the streets outside. As the soldiers carried the president's body into the Petersen House, they first tried the parlor door opposite the foot of the stair, but finding it locked, they moved on to the diminutive room at the end of the hall. (*Photo courtesy Library of Congress, Prints and Photographs Division*)

Above left: The HWLD as it appeared in a National Park Service brochure titled *Lincoln Museum and the House Where Lincoln Died* that first appeared in the 1940s and was reissued by the NPS for the next forty years. An excerpt from the brochure details, "Realizing that the removal of the President over the cobblestones to the White House would prove fatal, the surgeon ordered the dying man to be carried down the stairway and across the street into the home of William Petersen.... Mrs. Lincoln, overcome with grief, remained in the front parlor, occasionally going to the bedside of her stricken husband. A meeting of the Cabinet was held in the rear parlor and Secretary of War Stanton immediately began his investigation of the assassination." This image is noteworthy because of what is missing from other photos. The distinctive spider-web window has been covered by a tacky sign with the vague message "Invites You To His Sea Food Restaurant. Dine. Dance" featuring a silhouette of a well-dressed couple posed in a dance embrace. Also, the round Doric column support for the brownstone stoop has been replaced by a rigid square-cornered column from the Brutalist architecture movement that emerged in the mid-twentieth century. (*Author's collection*)

Above right: The photo on the left represents the front door of the HWLD that was featured on an official NPS brochure in 1965 and the image on the right is from the modern day. The brochure details, "Entering the building, visitors walk in the footsteps of the men who carried the dying President into the house. They proceed through the hallway to the front and back parlors and to the room in which Lincoln died.... In the front parlor are a horsehair sofa and a high-back rocking chair from the Lincoln home in Springfield, and corner whatnots and center table similar in appearance to those in the room on the night of the assassination. In the back parlor is a sofa also from the Lincoln home in Springfield. The center table resembles the one used by Cpl. James Tanner in taking notes from witnesses of the tragedy being interviewed by Secretary of War Stanton." (*Author's collection*)

Next page, above: This postcard photo depicts the room in which the president died as it appeared in the 1940s. The bed is a recreation; however, the pillow on display is one from that night, stained with the blood of Abraham Lincoln. Soon, a curved metal railing would be added to the doorway designed to lead visitors through the room and outside of the HWLD via the back stairs. The pillow would soon be covered with a clear plastic case for protection and remained on display for more than twenty years before being removed to the museum of relics housed in the basement of Ford's Theatre across the street. (*Author's collection*)

Below: The bed in which Abraham Lincoln died is on display in Chicago, Illinois, as part of the Charles Gunther collection of Lincoln relics. Evidence survives in newspaper articles and in the files of the NPS at the HWLD suggesting that negotiations were going on during Oldroyd's tenure as curator to bring the bed back to the HWLD. The *Chicago Sunday Tribune* of May 11, 1924 reported: "A few months before his death he (Gunther) promised Mr. Oldroyd he would restore the bed to the death room, but he died before he could fulfill the promise. Nor did his heirs fulfill it." This postcard dates from the 1940s and is captioned: "Chicago Historical Society-Replica of room and actual bed in which Lincoln died." (*Author's collection*)

Above left: On December 7, 1958, the Petersen House was closed to begin extensive structural rehabilitation and restoration work. This third renovation included replacing the front steps, tearing down two rooms added to the rear of the house, and removing concrete from the backyard and re-landscaping the courtyard. The rooms had been added by Curator Osborn H. Oldroyd sometime around 1900 to facilitate expanded display of his collection and it is believed that Oldroyd also paved the courtyard space sometime around 1920. The restoration, timed to coincide with the nationwide sesquicentennial celebration of Lincoln's birth, included the extensive sandblasting of the brick facade. It was completed at a cost of $30,000 and the building was reopened to the public on July 4, 1959. This image, captioned "General view of front after sandblasting & prior to water proofing & pointing," was taken on February 10, 1959 by NPS photographer by Abie Rowe. (*Photo courtesy National Park Service Ford's Theatre Historic Site archives*)

Above right: For the first time since the home was constructed over a century before, the distinctive curved sandstone steps, brownstone stoop, iron railing, boot scraper, and recently added utilitarian Brutalist support column were removed from the HWLD. The contracting firm of George C. Martin, located at 4842 Georgia Ave. NW, was hired to restore the shrine. The work was part of the Mission 66 program of the National Park Service, a ten-year program undertaken to dramatically expand Park Service visitor services in time for the fiftieth anniversary of the establishment of the Park Service in 1966. While Mission 66 was principally designed for infrastructure projects such as roads, utilities, and employee housing, many of the chief benefactors were interpretive facilities and visitor centers. Aside from this, the most thorough of the three HWLD renovations, the Mission 66 program also produced iconic landmarks like the Gateway Arch in St. Louis, Independence Mall in Philadelphia, and the Cyclorama Building at the Gettysburg National Military Park. (*Photo courtesy National Park Service Ford's Theatre Historic Site archives*)

According to the December 17, 1958 *Washington Post & Times Herald* newspaper, "The wall in the background will be reduced to a height of 8 feet, which was that of the original brick wall. The space between the wall and the house will become a garden." This image of the HWLD west elevation, captioned "Demolition of rear of building", was taken on December 17, 1958 by NPS photographer Abbie Rowe. (*Photo courtesy National Park Service Ford's Theatre Historic Site archives*)

This image, captioned "Demolition of 1899 Addition during 1959 Rehabilitation. Second Floor Bathroom has yet to be demolished" was taken on December 17, 1958 by NPS photographer Abbie Rowe. It offers an ideal image of the additions made to the HWLD dating from the decades following Lincoln's death in the building. According to the NPS official Historic Structure Report, the building at left (or south) was added in 1923, the building to the right (or north) was added in the 1870s, and the area in the center represents the 1899–1900 addition. On the roof at left the bathroom addition can be seen, this addition was added by the Petersen heirs in 1872. (*Photo courtesy National Park Service Ford's Theatre Historic Site archives*)

Above: One of the major changes of this renovation involved the reconfiguration of the route visitors utilized during tours of the HWLD. This image shows the rebuilt 1908 rear porch enclosure and newly added stairway to aid in the flow of visitors to the basement exit. According to the December 17, 1958 *Washington Evening Star* newspaper, "Entrance will be through the first-floor front door.... The route from there leads to-but not into-the Lincoln room, now fenced off, onto the back porch and down the stairs to the rear garden, then through the ground-floor hallway and out on 10th Street from beneath the front stoop. Next in line as part of Mission '66 is the restoration of Ford's Theater itself. While the rehabilitation of Petersen House cost $ 30,000, the theater will require about $ 1 million." This image, captioned "General view of rear after sandblasting & prior to water proofing & pointing" was taken on February 10, 1959 by NPS photographer Abbie Rowe. (*Photo courtesy National Park Service Ford's Theatre Historic Site archives*)

Below: This photo of the downstairs exit to the courtyard in rear of the HWLD was taken by the author on the 150th anniversary of Lincoln's death, April 15, 2015. This was the original back porch for the Petersen family, the Schade family, and the Oldroyd family. On this spot, homeowner William Petersen, moments after Lincoln's body was removed, played out one of the lesser known scenes of the aftermath. Petersen, incensed by the stinking piles of bloody bandages and leaking mustard plasters littering his home, stormed into the death room, grabbed the blood-stained pillow from atop the death bed, and tossed it out the window, terrifying the Ulke brothers. The pillow, possibly still wet with Mr. Lincoln's blood, landed on the fieldstone courtyard on this spot below. On May 4, 1865, an irate William Petersen sent the U.S. War Department a bill for $550 seeking compensation for the use of his home, furniture, and linens. Upon receipt of this unexpected bill, someone in the quartermaster general's office added a note reading: "Pay Mr. Petersen a reasonable sum for the property consumed and for the use of his house, and inform him that the War Department has no authority to pay anything further." Officials there decided that the "reasonable sum" was $293.50 for Mr. Lincoln's nine-hour stay.[9]

This photo of the room in which Abraham Lincoln died was taken on December 17, 1958 by NPS photographer Abbie Rowe. It offers one of the first views of the newly installed curved metal bronze topped balustrade railing at the right of the photo. A washbasin rests atop the tiered, marble-topped washstand at the foot of the bed. A chamber pot rests against the wall between the washstand and the rocking chair. The blood-stained relic pillow rests unprotected, covered only by a clean white cloth at the head of the reproduction bed. Two framed prints, one an engraving by John Frederick Herring, Sr., titled *The Village Blacksmith* hangs on the north wall and the other, a painting by Rosa Bonheur's titled *Horse Fair*, hangs above the bed, just as they were that fateful night. (*Photo courtesy National Park Service Ford's Theatre Historic Site archives*)

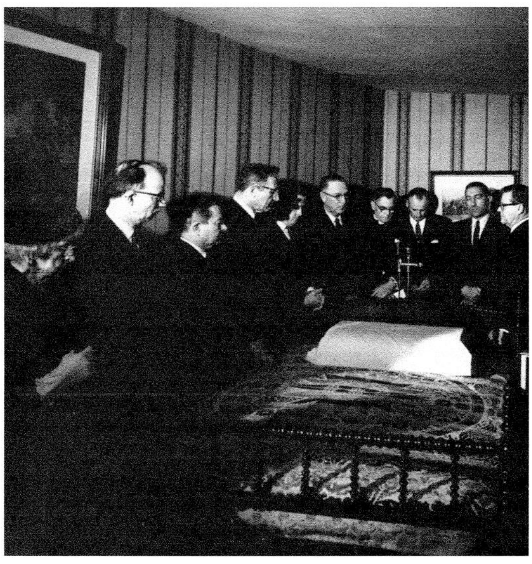

A photo taken by NPS photographer Jack Rottier on April 15, 1965, the 100th anniversary of Abraham Lincoln's death, with dignitaries gathered around the bed, eyes closed, and heads bowed in prayer. Included in this image are U.S. Secretary of the Interior Stewart Udall (second from right) and Milton Young, U.S. senator from North Dakota (fifth from right). The blood-stained pillow rests in a plastic case (covered by a clean white cloth for protection from ultraviolet light) at the head of the bed. (*Photo courtesy National Park Service Ford's Theatre Historic Site archives*)

Above: The Ulke photograph, described earlier in this volume, capturing the Lincoln deathbed and blood-stained pillow in the room in which Lincoln died, remained unknown for ninety-six years. Because Secretary of War Stanton was confiscating prints and negatives of assassination-related scenes, Ulke kept his photograph secret, passing it down through his family. In 1961, it was sold to Mrs. Dorothy Kunhardt for $3,750 by a ninety-three-year-old Ulke descendant known only as "Mrs. Easter," who donated the money to her church in England. This photo, taken by NPS photographer Jack Rottier on January 5, 1968, pictures NPS Central National Capital Parks Superintendent Monte E. Fitch (at left) accepting the famed photograph from Dorothy M. Kunhardt (second from right). (*Photo courtesy National Park Service Ford's Theatre Historic Site archives*)

Below: This image, taken in early 1968, depicts the room in which Lincoln died with the recently donated Kunhardt/Ulke photo in place on an easel at the foot of the bed. More importantly, the image offers a clear view of the Lucite box containing the pillow, stained with the blood of Lincoln, which had been handed down through, and donated by, members of the Petersen family. This pillow was one of several used under President Lincoln's head as he lay dying in the Petersen Boarding House. According to an affidavit dated May 26, 1950 and retained in the files of the HWLD at Ford's Theatre, the pillow was given to the NPS by the heirs of Mrs. Pauline Petersen Wenzing, daughter of William and Anna Petersen. (*Photo courtesy National Park Service Ford's Theatre Historic Site archives*)

Above: This photo, taken on September 9, 1971 by NPS photographer Jack Rottier, depicts guests passing through the room and stopping to look closely at the blood-stained pillow. For many years, the National Park Service maintained a guard in the room during regular business hours. The guard's sole duty was to watch over the sacred relic because, as witnessed by this photo, the pillow was within easy reach of every visitor. The otherwise empty room was being "watched" by an elderly uniformed guard who sat in the corner and was often found by visitors dozing off. There are a few photos that survive on the internet picturing youngsters taking advantage of this inattentiveness by climbing the rail and lying in the bed to have their picture snapped. Historic preservation during this era was obviously a shadow of what it is today. (*Photo courtesy National Park Service Ford's Theatre Historic Site archives*)

Below: In September 1978, restoration on the three rooms of the lower floor of the HWLD began. This photo, looking towards the entrance and down the long hallway, depicts the room in which Abraham Lincoln died taken during that time when the curved metal railing was absent while being refurbished. The ubiquitous *Village Blacksmith* framed print remains in place as well as other prints (*The Stable*, *Horse Fair*, and *The Barnyard*) that were all present on the walls that fateful night. Along with the change of metal railing, the carpet has been replaced by a new design more appropriate to that present that night. (*Author's collection*)

Above: On July 25, 1980, the restoration work was completed and the doors were once again opened to the public. Ironically, the 1980 restoration was done at the same cost as the 1958 restoration: $30,000. This photo of the room in which Abraham Lincoln died pictures the entrance to the HWLD in the background and features the newly reinstalled curved metal railing visible at right. More furnishings have been added to the room, including a camel back travel trunk with a Union Army soldier's kepi cap resting atop it in the lower left corner. "The high-back rocking chair is positioned near the foot of the bed in the exact spot where the Secretary of the Navy, Gideon Welles, sat in a similar rocking chair hour after hour throughout that long painful night."[10] A desk covered with writing materials, a photo album of CdV, a metal travelling box and books can be seen against the opposite wall. (*Author's collection*)

Below: This photo, taken of the room in which Lincoln died by the author on the 150th anniversary of his death (April 15, 2015), represents the room as it appears today. The 1980 restoration had, based on newspaper woodcuts made immediately after the tragedy, correctly moved the door 18 inches away from the exterior wall. In addition, an 1849 door (visible in this photo) was taken from the third floor to replace the reproduction door from 1932. The door, when opened, reveals a stairway to the basement from where it is believed that most of the water and supplies were retrieved during that fateful night. A 6-foot-tall glass partition screen was added to the iron railing in 2000 "to prevent visitors from touching or removing any objects from the death room ... due to the visitors' natural tendency to touch the bed and the wall above."[11] The reproduction furniture previously on display is now replaced by authentic period examples and the toilet articles seen positioned throughout the room were obtained from the National Park Service Furnishings Office at Harper's Ferry. (*Photo by author*)

Above: This photo, taken on December 6, 1966 by NPS photographer Abbie Rowe, pictures the back parlor arranged loosely in the configuration as it may have been on the night of the assassination. Here Secretary of War Edwin Stanton began the earliest investigation of the crime while President Lincoln lay dying just across the hall. The major differences in this setting are the large oil painting of Stanton over the fireplace, which was not present that night and the absence of the "unmade bed" noted in Oldroyd's diagram used by George and Huldah Francis as boarders. The windows on the rear wall looked out upon the porch and courtyard. The HWLD was placed on the National Register of Historic Places the same year that this image was made. (*Photo courtesy National Park Service Ford's Theatre Historic Site archives*)

Below: This photo, taken on December 6, 1966 by NPS photographer Abbie Rowe, pictures the front parlor after the Mission 66 renovation at the HWLD. Here Mary Lincoln wrestled with her grief as her husband lay dying down the hall. Since the room was used as the sitting room by the Francis family that fateful night, it has been decorated in a utilitarian fashion that the family might recognize with a dresser, sewing machine, washstand, bed, and community table in this busy little space. During the Schade family years, this space was used as an office for the *Washington Sentinel.* During the Oldroyd years, this was the first room visitors would be ushered into. It was full of Lincoln objects and relics, "On the walls are more pictures, mainly photographs, and extend to relatives and people and places closely associated with Mr. Lincoln. They include one of Lincoln's stepmother and his mother's brother, Dennis Hanks. Portraits of Lincoln's law partners are here with later pictures of himself and his Cabinet. Photographs of his wife are arrayed by themselves, and with them a lock of that lady's hair."[12] (*Photo courtesy National Park Service Ford's Theatre Historic Site archives*)

Above: This photo was taken in 1980 after interior restoration work was completed and the doors once again opened to the public. It pictures the front parlor as it looked at the time the Francis family was renting it. The only noteworthy addition is the large plastic interpretive sign placed on the table. George and Huldah Francis's bed has been placed as it was on the night that Lincoln died. Although the entire Petersen family bristled whenever they heard their home referred to as a "boarding house," there can be no denying that the home was in fact used for that purpose, especially during the Civil War. Aside from the many actors residing there while performing across the street at Ford's Theatre, other noteworthy boarders included Vice President John C. Breckinridge and Waller Bullock, Abraham Lincoln's uncle-in-law. Operating a boarding house (or at least publicly announcing it) fluctuated greatly in Washington in the mid-1800s. The City Directories in 1860 and 1864 each list about eighty boarding houses; more than double that number appear in the 1867 directory. At one time, the Petersens placed beds on the stair landings, which were rented out to short-term boarders. (*Photo courtesy National Park Service Ford's Theatre Historic Site archives*)

Below: This photo, also taken in 1980, offers a close-up of the new plastic interpretive sign with lettering large enough that it could be read by visitors from the central hallway as they passed through the HWLD. It reads: "In this bedroom, Secretary of War Stanton held several cabinet meetings, interviewed witnesses, and ordered the pursuit of the assassins." These new signs were a far cry from the succinct hand-lettered placards used by Curator Oldroyd to identify the objects contained in his museum. Unlike these NPS signs, which were designed to be viewed from afar, Oldroyd's small neatly lettered signboards were scattered among a fantastic menagerie of noteworthy artifacts. This allowed visitors the ability to wander freely through the two parlor rooms, pausing at will to study any artifact that caught their fancy. A few of Oldroyd's signs survive in the archives of the National Park Service Museum Resource Center in Landover Maryland. (*Photo courtesy National Park Service Ford's Theatre Historic Site archives*)

Right: This image of the front parlor of the HWLD was taken on July 14, 1932 by a staff photographer for the Office of Public Buildings and Public Parks of the National Capital. Five years after it was purchased by the government, Osborn Oldroyd's Lincoln collection was moved across the street to the basement of Ford's Theatre and placed under the supervision of the Welfare and Recreation Association of the Office of Public Buildings and Public Parks. The process of moving the Oldroyd collection out of the house where Lincoln died across the street to Ford's Theatre began on December 8, 1931 and completed by New Year's Day 1932. According to General Order No. 461 dated March 9, 1932 from the Office of Public Buildings and Public Parks of the National Capital, Oldroyd's collection "will hereafter be known and referred to as the "Lincoln Museum." On June 10, 1933, the Office of Public Buildings and Public Parks of the National Capital was abolished and its functions were transferred to the Department of the Interior and the National Park Service. (*Photo courtesy National Park Service Ford's Theatre Historic Site archives*)

Below: This 1980 NPS photo pictures the front parlor recreated to look as it did on the night of the Lincoln tragedy. The large plastic interpretive sign placed on the table in this room reads: "Between visits to her husband's bedside, Mary Lincoln waited in this parlor with her son Robert and friends of the Lincoln family." According to the NPS *Historical Handbook Series No. 3* from 1949, "The horsehair sofa and the high-back rocking chair in this room were once in the Lincoln home in Springfield. The sofa is in the same location as the one occupied by Mrs. Lincoln on the night of April 14 and the morning of April 15, 1865. The corner whatnots and center table are similar in appearance and in the same position as those in the room on the night of the assassination." (*Photo courtesy National Park Service Ford's Theatre Historic Site archives*)

Left: Another image of the opposite side front parlor of the HWLD taken on July 14, 1932 by a staff photographer for the Office of Public Buildings and Public Parks of the National Capital. According to the NPS *Historical Handbook Series No. 3* from 1949, "Two ornate vases, gifts of Lincoln to Caleb Blood Smith, are on the mantelpiece."[13] The small placard on the mantel visible in this image note the significance of the vases and their donor. The framed prints on the wall are Leonardo da Vinci's *The Last Supper* and David Bustill Bowser's portrait of Abraham Lincoln. The inclusion of Bowser's 1865 Lincoln portrait is symbolic due to the artist's standing as a nineteenth-century African-American ornamental artist, portraitist and designer of battle flags for eleven African-American regiments during the Civil War. Bowser was an artist whose "works were the first widely viewed, positive images of African Americans painted by an African American," according to his Pennsylvania Historical and Museum Commission marker in Philadelphia. (*Photo courtesy National Park Service Ford's Theatre Historic Site archives*)

Below: This 1980 NPS photo pictures the front parlor as it looked on the night of the Lincoln tragedy. Gone are the da Vinci and Bowser Lincoln prints, replaced by paintings of George Washington and his family, a snow sledding scene and Rosa Bonheur's titled *Horse Fair*, which can be found in earlier photos hanging above the bed in the room where Lincoln died. The vases from a half century before have been replaced by a pair of ornate candlesticks with a similar pedigree. According to the NPS *Historical Handbook Series No. 3* from 1949, "On the mantel are two candlesticks which were presented by Lincoln to Caleb Blood Smith, his Secretary of the Interior. The mantels and fireplaces in both the front and rear parlors are the originals."[14] The hands of the central clock on the mantel are forever frozen at 7:22 a.m., the exact moment of Lincoln's death. (*Photo courtesy National Park Service Ford's Theatre Historic Site archives*)

This photo was taken by the author during the sesquicentennial 150th anniversary commemoration of Lincoln's death on April 15, 2015. Ford's Theatre NPS Ranger Roger Powell places a wreath, with a sash reading "Department of the Interior National Park Service," in front of the house where Lincoln died. The Ford's Theatre Society and the National Park Service marked Abraham Lincoln's death at 7:22 a.m. with a wreath-laying ceremony accompanied by church bells tolling across the city, just as they did in 1865. Moments before the wreath was placed, actors offered testimony in the words of the participants and the Federal City Brass Band played Taps in the same spot at the exact moment of the president's death. Aside from Ranger Powell, author James Swanson, actor David Selby (of TV's *Dark Shadows* fame), Secretary of the Interior Sally Jewell, Director of Artistic Programming at Ford's Theatre Patrick Pearson, and actress Judy Williams are pictured. (*Photo by Alan E. Hunter*)

This 1980 NPS photo pictures the long hallway as it looked on the night of the Lincoln tragedy. The May 18, 1902 *Washington Times* magazine described the hallway during Oldroyd's tenure: "As one enters the doorway, he is ushered into a long hallway that runs past a small double parlor on the left, a stairway (to the upper floors) on the right and into a small bedroom in the far Northeast corner on the house. The entire lower floor of the Petersen House is occupied by the museum. The hall reveals several hundred framed pictures … every inch of its space covered with pictures of Lincoln before and after election, alone, and in the midst of his family. In this same hallway Major Henry Rathbone, feeling lightheaded and weak from loss of blood flowing from his gaping arm wound, collapsed and nearly died." (*Photo courtesy National Park Service Ford's Theatre Historic Site archives*)

A mid-1960s era photo of the HWLD offering an excellent view of the "Lincoln Cafe" restaurant adjoining the shrine. Gone are the striped tarpaulin awnings so prevalent in previous photos, replaced by enameled porcelain backed neon signs, so evocative of an era, but also so contextually out of place. Companies first began using neon gas signs such as these during the late 1920s and early 1930s to bring a little extra attention to their businesses. Although undoubtedly gaudy, neon signs were seen as bright, vivid, and alluring signage that was both affordable and attractive. Signs like these were scattered all around the district in bars, businesses, pharmacies—all keeping the streets bright at night. By the 1960s, when this photo was taken, people began to associate neon signs with shady businesses and, National Shrine or not, 10th Street began a slow decline. (*Author's collection*)

This photo dates from the 1980s and although the HWLD was still recognized as a shrine, by this time, both the Petersen House and Ford's Theatre were in a state of suspended disrepair. James Swanson, author of the seminal book *Manhunt: The 12-Day Chase for Lincoln's Killer* describes: "Every April 14, on the hour of the assassination of Abraham Lincoln, the place where it happened is one of the loneliest historical sites in America. I should know. I've been making disappointing anniversary pilgrimages to the scene for more than a quarter of a century." Swanson describes visits to the "then-seedy neighborhood surrounding Ford's Theatre" only to find no official commemoration of the historic event taking place there on this sad, yet important anniversary. Luckily, during the last two decades, the area has changed dramatically and the landmark has been restored to its former glory. (*Author's collection*)

It is easy to forget that from the moment that Lincoln died in this building, it was viewed as a Civil Rights landmark. Secretary of the Navy Gideon Welles, a close friend of Mr. Lincoln, wrote in his diary: "About 6 A.M. I experienced a feeling of faintness, and for the first time after entering the room a little past eleven I left it and the house and took a short walk in the open air.... Large groups of people were gathered every few rods, all anxious and solicitous.... The colored people especially-and there were at this time more of them perhaps, than of whites—were overwhelmed with grief."[15] When the Memorial Association of the District of Columbia first proposed placing a Lincoln museum in the building, they promoted it to Oldroyd as such. While it is true that the HWLD became somewhat of a *de facto* gathering place for African-Americans over the generations, it never translated into economic viability. This photo, titled "People outside the house where Lincoln died," was shot in December of 1937 by John Vachon, a New Deal agency photographer with the Farm Security Administration. The Great Depression spurred the rise of African-American activism and laid the groundwork for the Civil Rights Movement in the 1950s and 1960s. (*Author's collection*)

This large sized poster is from the *National Parks USA* series issued by the NPS in 1968 during the height of the Civil Rights movement in America. It depicts the house where Lincoln died as it looked in 1865. A broadside poster for the play *Our American Cousin* is plastered on the fence next to the distinctive spider-web window. A young African-American newsboy hawks newspapers from the sidewalk below the curved steps of the Petersen House. The building is unadorned with no hint of the event that is about to catapult it into historic immortality. (*Author's collection*)

Left: In August 1963 photographer Leonard Freed was in Washington, D.C., to hear Dr. Martin Luther King, Jr.'s "I Have a Dream" speech during the "March on Washington for Jobs and Freedom." His photographs of that historic day appeared in the book *This Is The Day: The March on Washington* and were on exhibit in August 2013 at the U.S. Library of Congress. This image, captioned, "An elderly white man and a young black man pass each other in front of the house where Lincoln died, where the former president was taken after being shot at Ford's Theatre across the street" illustrates Freed's recurring them of being "Black in White America". The government sign on the railing notes that admission to the HWLD was a dime, which hurt attendance in a city where so many other historic sites were free. (*Photo courtesy U.S. Library of Congress in Washington*)

Below: Martin Luther King, Jr., delivered his "I Have a Dream" speech from the steps of the Lincoln Memorial in Washington, D.C., to over 250,000 civil rights supporters on August 28, 1963. The speech was the defining moment of the civil rights movement and, alongside Lincoln's Gettysburg Address, remains one of the most iconic speeches in American history. In the wake of the speech and march, King was named "Man of the Year" by *TIME* magazine for 1963, and in 1964, he was the youngest person ever awarded the Nobel Peace Prize. (*Photo courtesy U.S. Library of Congress in Washington*)

This photo of the HWLD dates from the 1940s era. A description of the house where Lincoln died in an official guidebook issued by the National Park Service in 1937 states, "To this house, which is directly opposite the Lincoln Museum, the stricken President was carried on the night of his assassination. Here, in a room on the first floor, he died the following day, April 15, 1865. Long neglected, the house was purchased by the Federal Government in 1896. Apart from its historic association with Lincoln, the house is interesting as an attempt to reproduce the furnishings and atmosphere of a typical home of the 1860's."[16] In 1947, admission to the Lincoln Museum in Ford's theatre was 12 ¢ and admission to the Oldroyd Museum was 12 ¢, which meant every paid customer received a Lincoln head penny as change. (*Photo courtesy National Park Service Ford's Theatre Historic Site archives*)

In the 1950s, when this photo was taken, the Petersen House was still struggling to find its identity a generation after all of Oldroyd's relics had been moved across the street and into Ford's Theatre. To make matters worse, the structure was in severe need of a facelift. The roof was leaking, moisture was seeping through the bricks and into the basement walls. The distinctive curved flight of Seneca sandstone steps leading up and into the house were threatening to crumble away. Contrarily, the population of Washington, D.C., reached an all-time high of 802,178 during the decade of the 1950s with population split 65 percent white and 35 percent black.[17] By the next decade, the population fell as did the percentages: 763,956 total population with 54 percent black citizens *versus* 46 percent white. It could be said that at a time when Lincoln's vision of racial equality in the nation's capital city had been achieved, the house where he breathed his last lay wasting away. (*Photo courtesy National Park Service Ford's Theatre Historic Site archives*)

This photo of the deteriorating front steps of the HWLD, looking north from 10th Street, was taken on April 9, 1953 by NPS photographer Abbie Rowe. The original cast-iron curled cantilever boot scraper at the base of the railing is absent and the brownstone Doric column supporting the stoop is in obvious distress. In his Washington, D.C., news column "The Rambler … is clued in on restoration", columnist George Kennedy noted, "The curving brownstone steps to the high stoop, up which Lincoln was carried, will have to be replaced. They have become badly cracked and chipped. But we can use the same iron railings. They are in perfect condition." This image reveals the remaining scars of a June 3, 1928 incident when a sightseeing bus ran into the porch, causing $58.88 worth of damage to the steps and support columns. The image also affords a good view of the door to the English basement that, according to the NPS records, dates from 1916 during Oldroyd's occupation of the building. (*Photo courtesy National Park Service Ford's Theatre Historic Site archives*)

This photo was taken by the author on July 1, 2018 shortly after the HWLD reopened following its most recent renovation. The HWLD was closed from September 2017 to June of 2018. According to the NPS: "The work included replacing the existing fire suppression system, updating historic furnishings and wallpaper, and general preservation and maintenance work on the historic structure." The steps were repaired to their former glory; however, the distinctive cast-iron curled cantilever boot scraper at the base of the railing was permanently removed. A sturdier windowless white pine door has been set in place to the English basement. According to the NPS, the spider-web door was rebuilt in 1959 and that "85% of the original fabric was retained." However, the original 1865/1959 door was replaced in 1989 and discarded. (*Photo by author*)

Right: This photo, taken on December 6, 1966 by NPS photographer Abbie Rowe, pictures the front steps of the HWLD after the 1958–59 renovation. They were accurately recreated to look just as they did when the dying president's body was carried up and into the Petersen House. Upon closer examination, a crack can be seen sprouting from the corner of the marble slab holding the distinctive boot scraper in place at the foot of the stairs. The original boot scraper was removed and added to the Lincoln Museum's collection in 1943. A replacement was fabricated and remained in place throughout the 1960s. Soon this ordinary relic from an extraordinary event in American history would disappear forever. (*Photo courtesy National Park Service Ford's Theatre Historic Site archives*)

Below: This photo was taken by the author on July 1, 2018 shortly after the HWLD reopened following a six month renovation. Part of this restoration was detailed in 2002 as "Deterioration of Brownstone Steps and Platform due to exposure to airborn pollutants, heavy use by museum visitors, and freeze-thaw dynamic introduced by cast iron railings (corroding ends where imbedded into top of stone surface)." During the closure, the NPS developed a creative way to tell the thousands of visitors about what happened here without showing them inside the space where he died. Guests were invited to take a virtual tour of the Petersen House, including the front and back parlors and the bedroom where Lincoln died, by downloading an app to their smartphones. In the Petersen House app, visitors listened to first-person accounts that brought them back to the night of the tragedy. Unlike previous renovations, this closure, through use of technology, enhanced our twenty-first-century understanding of what happened at the Petersen House. The program remains in place today. (*Photo by author*)

Above left: In late 1985 and early 1986, a rare urban excavation took place at the Petersen House directly under the room where Lincoln died. The rotting floor boards were pulled up and more than 5,000 artifacts were unearthed spanning over 135 years of living in the home. The refuse included fragments of ceramic dishes, jugs and vases, tiny wine goblets, perfume bottles, and medicine jars, machine-cut nails, shoes, painted horse-hair covered plaster, mica sheets possibly used for window panes, children's ceramic marbles, and broken pencil stubs, a bone domino, tobacco pipe bowls, and stems, straight pins, needles, and buttons, and a lady's hair comb. Also found were remains of meals served in the Petersen boarding house, including bones of cows, pigs, chickens, and turkeys, some still bearing the marks of a butcher's knife. The excavation also uncovered three or four damaged glass microscope slides that once belonged to boarders Julius and Henry Ulke, the two amateur Smithsonian Institution entomologists who also took the famous photograph of the bed where Lincoln died. (*Photo from the Annapolis Capitol newspaper*)

Above right: According to the National Park Service, in February 1959, "The facade was sandblasted, repointed, and then waterproofed." Although the facelift was pleasing aesthetically, it came with an unintended consequence that threatens the longevity of the HWLD to this day. In a 2002 report, the NPS noted, "Rising damp within masonry walls remains a severe problem in several locations." These photos, taken by the author on July 1, 2018, reveal that not only were the bricks sandblasted and painted, so was the mortar. The mortar lines visible on the east front of the building are painted on. Not only is mortar's primary job to cushion load transfer from one irregular unit to another irregular unit, mortar should be more porous than the masonry units so that moisture in the wall, seeking the path of least resistance, will mostly travel through the mortar. Here, it can be seen that the moisture is traveling through the bricks instead, causing a honeycomb consistency that may threaten the load bearing properties of the bricks. In time, conceivably, the bricks may crumble and the HWLD will be no more. (*Photo by author*)

Above left: During the 1958–1959 restoration of the house, a metal lath mesh was used to repair major cracks in the plaster, like the one seen in this photo from that time, but this fix proved to be problematic. Moisture continued to seep through the walls causing the plaster to fail, in some cases spectacularly. The HWLD was restored by the NPS during 1979–80 when again, water seepage through the plaster and wallpaper caused the need for repair. The death room was particularly affected, and for obvious reasons, was the main focus of the repair but the damage was spread fairly evenly throughout the house. (*Photo courtesy National Park Service Ford's Theatre Historic Site archives*)

Above right: This photo of the English basement hallway and door to 10th Street, taken by the author on July 1, 2018, suggests that the moisture damage, vexing the house for so long, continues today. It should be remembered that the Petersen House was never intended to last forever. According to the Department of the Interior, "a Washington, D.C., newspaper article printed the week following President Lincoln's death, April 15, 1865, concern was expressed that, 'the frail Petersen House, built rather on tenement style, would not long stand as a memento of the great man who died in it.' Despite the concern of more than a century ago, the house at 516 10th Street N.W. Washington, D.C., has endured in its original state and is now a National Shrine." Americans owe a debt of gratitude to the pioneering conservation efforts of the Memorial Association of the District of Columbia, Curator Osborn H. Oldroyd, the War Department, the Welfare and Recreational Association of Public Buildings and Grounds and the National Parks Service for their stewardship and care of the HWLD. (*Photo by author*)

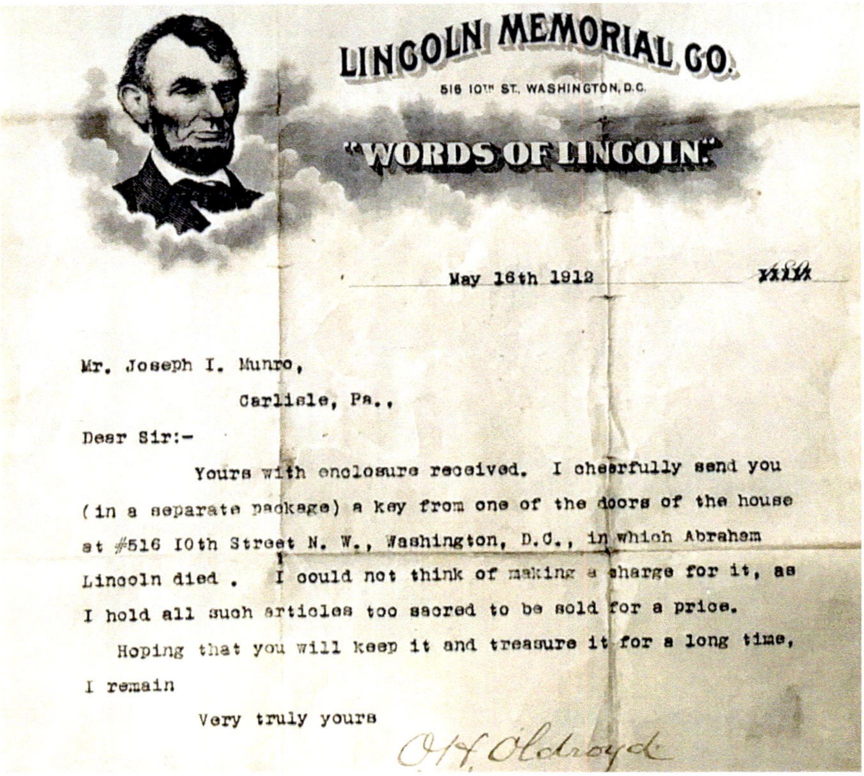

LINCOLN MEMORIAL CO.

516 10TH ST. WASHINGTON, D.C.

"WORDS OF LINCOLN."

May 16th 1912

Mr. Joseph I. Munro,

Carlisle, Pa.,

Dear Sir:-

Yours with enclosure received. I cheerfully send you (in a separate package) a key from one of the doors of the house at #516 10th Street N. W., Washington, D.C., in which Abraham Lincoln died. I could not think of making a charge for it, as I hold all such articles too sacred to be sold for a price.

Hoping that you will keep it and treasure it for a long time, I remain

Very truly yours

O.H. Oldroyd

This letter, found in the collection of the Smithsonian Institution, accompanies a simple, yet important, relic of the HWLD. On the ornate letterhead of the "Lincoln Memorial Company" headquartered in the Petersen House, it is dated May 16, 1912 and addressed to a collector from Carlisle, Pennsylvania. "I cheerfully send you (in a separate package) a key from one of the doors of the house at # 516 10th Street N.W., Washington, D.C., in which Abraham Lincoln died. I could not think of making a charge for it, as I hold all such articles too sacred to be sold for a price. Hoping that you will keep it and treasure it for a long time, I remain, very truly yours, O.H. Oldroyd." (*Photo by author*)

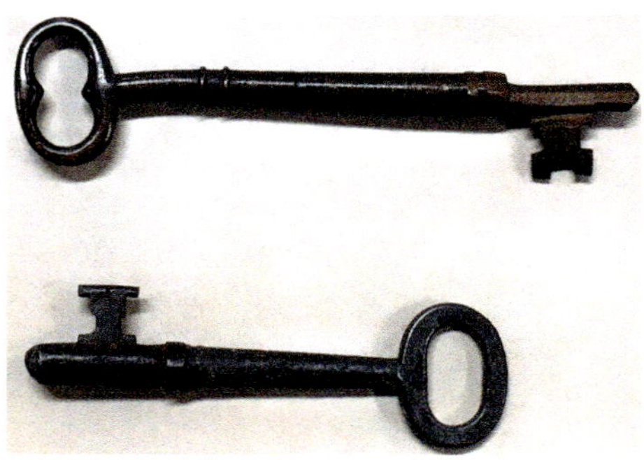

These keys, accompanied by the above letter and likewise found in the collection of the Smithsonian Institution, represent the most common of household objects connected to the first great tragedy in American presidential history. These otherwise ordinary skeleton keys illustrate the commitment to the conservation of objects by the country's first Lincoln museum curator, the common collector and our nation's longest serving guardian of objects, the Smithsonian Institution. During Oldroyd's day, the collecting of objects was considered folly and placed in the genre of a carnival sideshow, a mere cabinet of curiosities. Today, these same objects are held sacred in the chronology of our cultural history and, when not housed in a museum, remain in high demand by amateur collectors. The preservation of the house where Lincoln died is among the most precious of those American relics. It remains integral to Abraham Lincoln's rise to secular sainthood. (*Photo by author*)

EPILOGUE

Americans were stunned by the assassination of Abraham Lincoln. How could this have happened? Who could have perpetrated such a horrible crime? Did the assassin act alone? These questions have been repeatedly asked in the century and a half since the Lincoln assassination. However, there was one question in particular asked after the death of President Lincoln that does not crop up in similar events over that same time frame. That is the question of the selection of the place where Lincoln died. In the years immediately following the president's death, there were many who questioned the dignity of Lincoln's death in a tiny ordinary room, occupied by a common soldier in the rear of a public boarding house.

It is well known that after Lincoln was shot inside Ford's Theatre, surgeons determined that the gravely wounded man would not survive the rough and bumpy trip to the White House, even though it was less than a mile way. Initially, it was suggested that Lincoln be taken to Taltuval's saloon next door to Ford's Theatre, where the assassin Booth had braced himself with a drink before the murder. "It was the proprietor who discouraged the idea. 'Don't bring him in here,' he ordered. 'It shouldn't be said that the President of the United States died in a saloon.'"[1] A split-second decision was made to bring the dying man into the home of the William Petersen across the street. And so it was that in a humble bedroom of this structure, on the morning of April 15, 1865, Abraham Lincoln died.

Over the succeeding generations, historians have helped to put the question of the choice of Willie Clark's room in the Petersen House into perspective. In Petersen's eyes, his home was an upper-class dwelling with rooms to rent to men of means in the Capital City. After all, Petersen could count among his former borders three former U.S. congressmen—Andrew K. Hay and William A. Newell of New Jersey and John C. Breckinridge of Kentucky, who would go on to become James Buchanan's vice president from 1857 to 1861. Newspapers were less kind, describing the Petersen home as a common boarding house. The startling turn of events that April night, coupled with the public disdain that followed, undoubtedly contributed to William Petersen's 1871 death and that of his wife's demise from undisclosed causes exactly four months later. But for the death of Abraham Lincoln, William Petersen was destined to disappear from the pages of history, remembered only as the former owner of the south half of Lot 14 on square 347 in the District of Columbia.

In time, the story of the Petersen House became less about the former owner and more about the man who died there. "It was no bigger than a log cabin, the length of three

This CdV photo of *The Village Blacksmith* dates from the Civil War era and is from the author's collection.

tall men lying down head-to-toe, and much narrower.... Already cramped with a bureau, table, and eight or nine chairs on a very warm Brussels carpet."[2]

> It would seem that the fates wanted the Great Emancipator to die amid humble surroundings, as were those of his infancy and youth, for the house wherein he breathed his last was not an imposing structure, even in the '60's. It is a three storied, narrow, brick building. When the dying president was taken there, it was a lodging home, and the room to which he was carried was among the humblest in the dwelling. It is a narrow room at the end of the first-floor hall; it was taken probably because of its convenience.[3]

As the pages of time continued to turn, people began to come around to the thought that the Rail-Splitter left this earth in a room no bigger than that from which he had come into it.

One of those "common" elements associated with the death of President Lincoln is an object that appears in every depiction of the death scene, whether pencil, ink, paint, charcoal, woodcut, photograph, or eyewitness account. It is a large framed print adaptation of a painting by artist John Frederick Herring known as *The Village Blacksmith*. The scene was inspired by Henry Wadsworth Longfellow's poem of the same name. The painting depicts a most ordinary blacksmith shoeing a horse with his dog obediently standing nearby. He glances over his shoulder to see his wife, holding a food basket in her arms, who has just entered the shop. Artist George Patterson's 1858–59 engraving of the painting stood silent witness on the wall above the dying president.

Today, each side of 10th Street N.W., between E and F in Washington, D.C., are restored as they were in 1865. Ford's Theatre and the Petersen House constitute the "Ford's Theatre National Historic Site." Operated by the National Park Service in partnership with the Ford's Theatre Society, both buildings exist for the purpose of educating the public about Lincoln's last hours. Standing as they are today, it is sometimes difficult to imagine that, historically, they have not always been dedicated to serving Lincoln's memory. In fact, it was not until several years after Lincoln's death that an effort was made to commemorate these buildings in any way. The modern museums of Ford's Theatre and the Petersen House started off quite humbly as silent structural memorials. A visit to the house where Lincoln died today allows each visitor the opportunity to walk through the first floor and stand inside the tiny, dimly-lit, otherwise insignificant room with the slanted ceiling where the last, best hope of a nation was lost.

ENDNOTES

Introduction

1 Dickens, C., *The Fireside Dickens: American Notes* (New York Oxford American Press American Branch, 1842).
2 Seneca sandstone is a rich, dignified color; it also has the unique property that it is relatively soft and easy to cut when it is taken out of the ground but hardens after the cut stone is set in place, making for an excellent building material. The steps were cut from the Aquia Creek quarry near Stafford, Virginia, considered to be the first quarry to be used heavily in constructing early Washington. Peck, G., *The Smithsonian Castle and the Seneca Quarry* (Charleston, S.C.: The History Press, 2013).
3 Boyd's Washington D.C. and Georgetown City directory, W.H. Boyd publisher, 1864.
4 Canavan, C., *Lincoln's Final Hours* (University Press of Kentucky, 2015).

The House Where Lincoln Died

1 United States Department of the Interior, National Park Service Informational Circula IV.
2 Reynolds, L. G., *Lincoln's Last Night*, including Carl Bertsch account.
3 *Washington Sunday Star*, January 24, 1909.
4 Albert Berghaus was an American illustrator from the 1860s–1890s. He worked principally for *Frank Leslie's Illustrated Newspaper*, producing sketches and wood engravings of important events during and after the Civil War.
5 Herman Faber is considered a pioneer of medical illustration in America. During the Civil War, he did many illustrations for the U.S. Army's six-volume *Medical and Surgical History of the War of the Rebellion*, but his most famous illustrations were those of Lincoln on his deathbed.
6 Alonzo Chappel (1828–1887) was a New York artist, best known for paintings depicting personalities and events from the American Revolution and early nineteenth-century American history.
7 Chase, S. B., *A Brief Study of Historic Exterior Paint on Windows*, Design Development Report; Ford's Theatre and Petersen House, (Alexandria, Va.: John Miliner and Associates, Inc. August 6, 2001).
8 National Park Service, "ARCHAEOLOGY AND HISTORIC PRESERVATION: Secretary of the Interior's Standards and Guidelines."
9 Office of the Quartermaster General, Consolidated Correspondence File, 1794–1915, Old Box 568, Lincolniana, NARA.

10 Allen, J. D., (HWLD curator) *Country Beautiful* magazine, December 12, 1966.
11 "William A. Petersen House. House Where Lincoln Died," Historic Structure Report National Park Service. U.S. Department of the Interior, 2002. Authors, Architrave P.C. Architects 420 Tenth St. SE, Washington, D.C., 2003.
12 *Washington Times* magazine, May 18, 1902, p. 2.
13 Caleb Blood Smith (April 16, 1808–January 7, 1864) was a U.S. Representative from Indiana and Lincoln's Secretary of the Interior from 1861 to 1863.
14 Since the time of this photo, considerable doubt has been raised by researchers for the National Park Service based on the appearance of the fireplaces' styles and designs as being more accurately fitted to the Victorian era rather than to the Civil War era.
15 Gideon Welles Papers, Diaries, 1824–1869 (Reels 1–5) Library of Congress.
16 Glimpses of Historical Areas East of the Mississippi River Administered by the National Park Service. United States Government Printing Office Washington, D.C., 1937.
17 Dodd, D. B., *Historical statistics of the United States: Two centuries of the census*.

Epilogue

1 Reck, W. E., *A. Lincoln: His Last 24 Hours* (McFarland & Company, Inc.: 1987).
2 Pitch, A. S., *They Have Killed Papa Dead! The Road to Ford's Theatre, Abraham Lincoln's Murder, and the Rage for Vengeance* (Hanover, New Hampshire: Steerforth Press, 2008).
3 Ulm, A. H., "In the House Where Abraham Lincoln Died and the Sixty-Two Year Quest for Mementoes of the Great Emancipator," *The Ford International Weekly*, *The Dearborn Independent*, Dearborn, Michigan, February 11, 1922.

BIBLIOGRAPHY

Articles/Newspapers

Getzinger, K., "Anne Petersen: Her Life in Washington, D.C. and the Petersen Boarding House (The House Where Lincoln Died. 1819–1871)," Washington, D.C., Ford's Theatre files, 2000

Menz, K. B., "The Lincoln Home-Historic Furnishings Report," Springfield, Illinois Lincoln Home National Historic Site, November 1, 1983

Olszewski, G. J., "House Where Lincoln Died: Furnishing Study," Washington, D.C., Division of History, Office of Archeology & Historic Preservation, National Park Service, Department of Interior, April 15, 1967

Peleszak, C., "Structural Report on the Petersen House (House Where Lincoln Died)," Washington, D.C., National Park Service, 1987

Taylor, D., and Ramirez, K., "The Memorials on Tenth St.," BoothieBarn.com blog post, March 24, 2014

Ulm, A. H., "In the House Where Abraham Lincoln Died and the Sixty-Two Year Quest for Mementoes of the Great Emancipator," *The Ford International Weekly*, *The Dearborn Independent*, Dearborn, Michigan, February 11, 1922

Virta, M. R., "Archeology of the Petersen House: Unearthing an Alternate History," Washington, D.C., Regional Archeology Program, National Park Service, National Capital Region, 1991

Books

Bain, R. T., *Lincoln's Last Battleground. A Tragic Night Recalled* (Bloomington, Indiana: Author House, 2005)

Benham, W. B., *Life of Osborn H. Oldroyd. Founder and Collector of Lincoln Mementos* (Washington, D.C.: William Burton Benham, 1927)

Buckingham, J. E., *Reminiscences and Souvenirs of the Assassination of Abraham Lincoln* (Washington, D.C.: Press of Rufus H. Darry, 1894

Holzer, H., and Williams, F. J., *Lincoln's Deathbed in Art and Memory: The "Rubber Room" Phenomenon* (Gettysburg, Pennsylvania: Thomas Publications, 1998)

Mathews, Jr., J. T., *History of the Lincoln Museum. The Ford Theatre and the Oldroyd collection* (Washington, D.C.: National Park Service, 1935)

McClure, S. W., *The Lincoln Museum and the House Where Lincoln Died* (Washington, D.C.: National Park Service, 1949)

National Park Service, *Ford's Theatre and the House Where Lincoln Died* (Washington, D.C.: National Park Service, 1969)

Oldroyd, O. H., *The Lincoln Memorial: Album Immortelles* (New York: G. W. Carleton & Co.; London: S. Low, Son & Co., 1883); *A Soldier's Story of the Siege of Vicksburg: From the Diary of Osborn H. Oldroyd* (Springfield, Illinois: H. W. Rokker, Printer, Binder and Stereotype, 1885); *A Tribute to the Memory of John A Logan from the Home of Lincoln* (Springfield, Illinois: O. H. Oldroyd, 1887); *Words of Lincoln: Including Several Hundred Opinions of his Life and Character by Eminent Persons of This and Other Lands* (Washington, D.C.: O. H. Oldroyd, 1895); *Lincoln's campaign; or, The Political Revolution of 1860* (Chicago: Laird & Lee, 1896); *The March to Victory: The Great Republican Campaigns of 1860 and 1896* (Chicago: Laird & Lee, 1896); *The Assassination of Abraham Lincoln: Flight, Pursuit, Capture, and Punishment of the Conspirators* (Washington, D.C.: O. H. Oldroyd, 1901); *The Poets' Lincoln: tributes in verse to the martyred President* (Boston, Mass.: Chapple Pub. Co., 1915)

Swanson, J. L., *Manhunt: The 12-Day Chase to Catch Lincoln's Killer* (New York, N.Y.: HarperCollins, 2006)

Reck, W. E., *A. Lincoln: His Last 24 Hours* (McFarland & Company, Inc.: 1987)

About the Author

ALAN E. HUNTER is a former officer and board member of the Indiana National Road Association and is active in Irvington Historic Society. He has co-authored two books on the Irvington community of Indianapolis and two books on the Historic Indiana National Road in 2013. He has also authored another three books on Indianapolis and the Irvington community. For over a decade, Hunter has written a weekly pop culture and history column for the *Weekly View* newspaper in Irvington. Hunter's articles have led to guest appearances on the History Channel, Discovery Channel, ESPN, NBC Sports, and many other local and national news programs. For the past twenty years, Hunter has led talks and programs in Irvington that have collected food and personal care items for the Irvington homeless shelter, gathering well over two tons of food, clothing, and personal care goods for distribution. A former teacher and baseball coach at Westfield High School, he graduated from Indiana University and has been married to his wife, Rhonda, for over thirty years. They have two children, daughter, Jasmine, and son, Addison, and a little rescue dog named Ace (Acey).